This Is Not My Story

Healing through Acceptance, Action, and Ascension

LORRAINE C. LORDI

ISBN: 0615502792
ISBN-13: 9780615502793

FOR MY AUTHOR

CONTENTS

Acknowledgments: ix

Chapter One: Why Write It Now?   1

Chapter Two: Who Could Believe a Truth
                    that Wacky?   11

Chapter Three: But I Don't Want to Write about It.   19

Chapter Four: OK, Then – You Write It.   27

Chapter Five: Hey, Buddy, I Really Don't Like
                    the Way Your Story is Going.   37

Chapter Six: The Answer You Seek Is
                    Simple, My Dear.   51

Chapter Seven: How I Look on the Outside
                    Isn't Anywhere Close to How
                    I Feel on the Inside.   61

Chapter Eight: Major Shifts Within Have To
                    Happen Within the Layers Before
                    the Surface Can Change.   71

Chapter Nine: Frozen up from My Heart to My Soul.   81

Chapter Ten: Either Heal Me or Send Someone
                    Whose Love Will Help Me Get
                    Through This.   95

Chapter Eleven: I'm Not There Yet. . .   109

Chapter Twelve: But At Least I'm Still Here.   117

PHOTOGRAPHS

The following photographs were taken at the Abbey of Gethsemani in Trappist, Kentucky.

"First Morning" (cover)
"After the Rain"
"Perigree Moon in Bare Spring Branches"
"Moon Rocks Deep in the Woods"
"End of Day"
"Darkness in the Garden"
"Waiting"
"Two Trees at Daybreak"
"Great Silence"
"A Path to Somewhere"
"The Road Back Home"
"Beyond Words"

The following photograph was taken in Ruleville, Mississippi.

"Easter Morning"

ACKNOWLEDGEMENTS

This book would not have been possible without my close friend, mentor, and editor, Alison Gaynor. Nearly forty years ago (forty years – yikes!), the two of us slouched on barstools in a seedy beer joint in South Bend, Indiana talking about literature, life, and that guy on our literary magazine who was still fuming because Alison became editor and I, her assistant. Even all those years ago, Alison had an incomparable eye for revision and an astute manner that was both straightforward and reassuring. Along with her husband, Mark, she formed her own editing business in Illinois, and no one anywhere can match her expertise. I have to give her added thanks, too, for reading this manuscript that probably didn't fit into her way of thinking. She's a pragmatist; I'm an idealist. She's down-to-earth; I'm head-in-the-clouds. Despite these differences, she spent countless hours getting this book to where it was supposed to be. We don't sit on barstools any more, but when Alison comes to Boston, I promise to buy her lobster.

To all the people in this book as well as those hiding in the spaces between words and lines, my deepest thanks. I would not be here, filled with such faith, hope, and courage if it weren't for you.

And to Emily, Joe, Catherine, Sam, and Jeff, what can I say? There are no words, really, to express how deeply grateful I am to you for all the many gifts you bring into my life. I suppose "I love you" works, but even that doesn't seem good enough.

WHY TELL IT NOW?

This is not a book I want to write.

In fact, I have been putting this writing off for more than two years. Maybe before now, I was too afraid. Or angry. Or sad. Or doubtful. Or something that goes along with being in a chapter of my life in which I have little control. A chapter I never anticipated. Or asked for. Or wanted.

If I were going to spend my time writing a book, I would not obsess over writing the great American novel (I'm pretty sure that's already been done), but I'd work on writing a pretty good one. One that even people outside of my friends and family would say, "Hey, this is all right. You should read it sometime."

Or I'd write a collection of gripping short stories filled with intriguing characters who are (as we all are at some point in our lives) caught between the near tragedies of living and the happily-ever-afters. (Actually, I have started this project, and hope to finish it someday – that is, when this book, which I really don't want to write, finds its way to its final punctuation mark.)

But now feels like the right time to put fear and fiction aside and write the truth as best as I can. Why now? Because I believe

I've come to new truths about pain and suffering that make sense to me. These insights have also made my heart feel lighter and more hopeful instead of feeling empty and dark. To be honest, though, the thought of exposing beliefs both personal and spiritual frightens me down to my ever-tingling toes.

I am a private person. I am also no theologian. As far as religions and mysteries outside of this physical world go, I feel people have the right to believe whatever they choose. There may be one mountaintop, but there are, as the wise among us say, many pathways to get there.

Yet these startling truths in my life have become so real, so powerful as of late, that they have erased my fears as to how these words will be received. Of course, I hope that the insights in this book resonate with a few if not many readers. But in the end, that doesn't matter, really. I've only been asked to offer these concepts, not worry about how others may react. As my good friend Jean Starr said to me, "Lorraine, don't worry. God doesn't call the equipped. He equips the called."

I certainly hope she's right because I feel about as capable of taking on this new writing journey as a mountain climber facing Mount Everest without shoes, poles, or a compass. Regardless of my ineptness, though, the mountain stands there before me. What else can I do but nod humbly and begin the ascent? I've been sitting down here at its base in the shadows for too long.

So I'll take a deep breath and dare to tell what I've learned through my own physical challenges over these past two years — challenges that aren't meant to be compared to anyone else's. As Holocaust survivor Elie Wiesel said, when it comes to individual suffering, we cannot compare. We can only sympathize, for what affects one's heart is at the same time both personal and universal. And so, for me, the lessons I'm learning about my own suffering begin with this premise:

All that's going on down here — this thing we call life — is a great book already written for each of us. All we have to do in order to realize happiness, which is our natural state, is to turn our plans over to the Great Author of our story and say, "All right then, Whoever and Whatever You are. I'll be Your main character. Just give me the grace — and an overflowing supply of courage — to hear Your words. Because it's not so easy, you know, to walk along on a path that stretches out farther than I can see."

Being the character instead of the writer is a terrifically humbling concept to grasp. Especially for a writer and a person like me who used to think — and sometimes still does — that I'm in control of my destiny. The captain of my own ship, as the poet says. As my ego likes to tempt me, I am that great. That powerful. That almighty.

But with a lot of head and heart work in facing the dark voices that consciously and unconsciously blur my attention to this greater power, I've learned to recognize that ego-voice. And I have come to know this truth: My ego never has and never will have my best interests at heart.

By working on changing my perspective through a process that probably won't end until my life here on earth ends, I've learned to look that ego "it's all about me" in the eye and say, "No, this isn't about me. So ego, head out the back door so that I can turn my attention to a higher, more lovable Source for my well-being and happiness." This is not an offer I'm making. It is an order.

Once the ego slinks away, the Real Author who has been patiently whispering to me all these years can come inside my heart and coach me. And boy, do I need coaching because now this Author adds this crazy twist to the mix: "Oh, and another thing, Lorraine. Allowing Me to be the author of your story, however hard it may seem at times, is a good thing. Rather magnificent, in fact."

But before we can accept that upside-down way of looking at life – that we are not the creators of our own destinies nor are we puppets in the hands of an incompetent, careless writer – we have to do something even harder. Some might call this step near impossible. I once did. Sometimes I still do.

We have to take a huge leap out of the reality we have created for ourselves and trust that this story, which is not ours, is written out of great love for us. It's no easy matter to wrap your arms around an idea like that. Especially when you find yourself stumbling in the darkness without one tiny star in the night sky to offer you a glimmer of hope.

I know. Because over these past four years, I've stumbled and crashed down like that – literally as well as figuratively – more than a few times.

("It's been so hard lately. Some days I can't even get off of the couch. I lie there, staring at the walls, feeling nothing. I try to care about something, anything. But it's like I'm numb to everything that once mattered. An empty shell whose inside life has stagnated. Lately, too, I've been feeling like I'm standing on the brink of a bridge on the darkest night of the year."

I shared these dark thoughts in a late night call last January to my son Joe.

"Don't even say that, Mom. It's not funny."

"I know it's not funny, Joe. But it's the truth. I know what I just admitted is a frightening thought, but I just had to tell someone because I don't think it's good for me to keep how I've been feeling buried inside any longer.")

Teetering on a bridge and jumping are two different matters altogether. But this depth of despair looms as an especially contrary idea for a person like me who has always managed to find a rosy reason for every difficulty in my life.

("So what if my new car is totaled, honey? At least you and I are standing out here without a scratch on us." The teenage girl who plowed her father's monster truck into my little red car three days before Christmas continued crying.

"But look at your car." She sobbed louder. I glanced over at my car. It looked like a crumpled tomato soup can. I smiled at her and shrugged my shoulders. "Cars can be fixed. Other things can't. Don't worry. It will be all right." Then I gave her a hug and stood in the cold with her until her family came to take her home.)

So for me, the "too much mustard for the hot dog, Pollyanna in the group," just the mere thought of leaning out on the rusty rail of an abandoned bridge above a bottomless pit showed me the extent to which sorrow and anger and despair had overtaken my former positive self. The self I knew before this unexpected chapter entered into my life. Or, as you could say, before I entered into it.

Somehow, though, (in part because I finally had the courage to speak my despair and weakness out loud to my son) I moved away from that cliff and never went back. I have crept back close. But I've never gotten more than a step or two before realizing that this is not the plot line I am meant to follow.

The new story line I'm listening to asks me to make the choice to stand up and step back from that bridge. To choose hope over despair. To choose not knowing over knowing. To choose accepting the questions instead of having all – or any – of the answers. To choose gratitude for what I have in my life instead of anger and despair over what I have lost. To choose happiness over sorrow. To choose love over fear.

So that's why I am writing this book. Not because I have the only solutions to life's challenges. Nor am I writing it because I am so good or so great or so exceptional. Believe me, I'm no saint. I'm writing it because Father Damien (you'll meet him soon) said that since I had a passion for writing, I was being called upon to share my experience of being diagnosed with a degenerative disease four years ago. To let other people who have come up against their own challenges share in my own journey. It might help, he said.

It's taken me a long while to get there. But through a bumbling up-and-down process, I'm finally beginning to learn. If I'm going to live my life fully and keep hope alive in my heart, I have to choose to believe this unseen and unverifiable concept:

No matter how bleak some chapters in my life appear, the Great Author of my story (or Creator, Loving Mother, Gentle Father, Holy Spirit, Lovingkindness, Faithful Friend, Allah, Guide, Luck, Almighty God, Yahweh, Serendipity, Abba, Truth, Compassion, Wholeness, Nothingness, Composer, Teacher, Breath, Best Buddy, Lover – choose whatever term works for you) intends great joy and peace and love for me. And for you, too. Always and without fail. Today, tomorrow, forever.

On my own, I could never have realized this truth that Someone has written every act in my life out of unsurpassed love for me.

On my own, I couldn't have even imagined, much less embraced this "What, are you some kind of nut living in La-La Land?" notion that goes against everything our American culture teaches us about the importance of being independent and powerful.

Yet here's the most remarkable thing: Once this truth comes to you – that your story is written out of love for you – you may come to see that everything, especially every human encounter, happens for a reason. And that reason is always for your well-being. Whether you can see it at the time or not.

You know that woman who noticed you today in the grocery store? You were passing each other in the health food aisle when you both picked up unsalted pumpkin seeds. She smiled at you. You smiled back. Although chances are you will never see her again, you felt a connection, a lightness of heart in sharing something as simple as unsalted pumpkin seeds. Also, in that moment, you forgot your own troubles. It may have seemed like an insignificant encounter, but for the rest of the day, you carried that smile somewhere inside of you whether you were aware of it or not.

Then, too, I remember one high school friend who stayed by my side when all my other friends abandoned me. These ins and outs of groups happen all the time during our teenage years. My experience was not unique. But this one friend, Debbie, was exceptional. During a cold, dark spell when I felt most alone living with my dad, she became my springtime.

More than once, Debs came over to stay with me when Dad was passed out in the living room with a glass of Dewar's next to his plate of cold meatloaf on the end table beside him. Quietly, so as not to disturb him, we snuck into the kitchen where she made Swiss cheese and mustard sandwiches on Wonder Bread.

I made big glasses of chocolate milk with extra gobs of Hersey's syrup.

Then we tiptoed up to my room, sat on my bed, and agreed that this meal was the most delicious combination in the entire world, and we were the only ones who knew about it. During those many nights together, we talked and laughed and listened to all those sappy '60s breakup songs and sang along with them. She carried the main melody in "Don't Let the Sun Catch You Crying" while I harmonized. She hummed while I sang the lead in "Yesterday."

I haven't seen Debbie in more than 20 years. I may never see her again. But whenever I hear someone order Swiss cheese on a sandwich or hear those two songs playing on the radio, I remember her with a gratitude that lifts me out of my present woes. When I remember Debs, I have no doubt: Despite all the disappointments and darkness in the world, there really is such a thing as a genuine friend to help you stand up when your own legs give out on you.

Being aware of those synchronistic encounters, however far off, fleeting, or forever, ultimately moves us closer to becoming the happy, joyful, free people we were always meant to be. The people we started out as in the first place. Except that in the chaos and ennui of everyday living, we inevitably lose track of who we are to begin with. That forgotten part of us I call the "soul." Or "innocence." Or "truth."

Then again, as far as delving into the layers of all the discoveries I made along this journey, I had little say as to when and where I might meet up with these new insights. As always seems to happen, truth tapped me on my shoulder when I least expected it. It appeared in the form of a grumpy-looking (but gentle as snow flurries) monk with strong, thick hands and light blue eyes that reflected a light from somewhere other than this earth.

So let me share with you this first unplanned meeting with this humble monk, Father Damien. It was he who so matter-of-factly introduced me to the truth that this is not my story.

(Oh, and good news: It's not your story, either.)

WHO COULD EMBRACE A
TRUTH THAT WACKY?

In my previous seven retreats at the Abbey of Gethsemani in Trappist, Kentucky, I never stayed after breakfast – an overflowing bowl of oatmeal with raisins and brown sugar – to listen to the brief talks by the Guestmaster. I had better things to do. Like skip two steps at a time up to my room, change into my running shoes and hiking pants, and head out to the hundreds of acres of footpaths where I could journey to places no one else had ever ventured before. Or so I imagined.

All alone on trails, marked and unmarked, I ran or walked as far as I could. I always stayed within the sound of the Abbey bells that chimed every fifteen minutes (except for that one time I got lost and literally, like the infamous bear of song, went over the mountain. But that story comes later.) Hearing the bells reminded me when it was time to get back for noon prayers – and the main meal of the day.

But then after that vegetarian meal of potatoes, rice, or pasta, I headed out again in an opposite direction. I traveled somewhere else the hills beckoned – maybe up the path to Crater Lake to watch a red-tailed hawk sailing effortlessly above the earth. The hawk never seemed lonely being up there by itself. But sometimes, when another hawk floated into the same space, these well-known loners had the gift of appreciating aloneness along with solitude. Together yet separate – these hawks somehow knew this invaluable secret to wholesome relationships.

Many times, I trekked miles to the deserted stone cabin whose tin roof was blanketed with ivy. The story goes that this one room hermitage with two windows and a fireplace was built for a monk who wanted to live out his life in total solitude. But once the house was ready, he changed his mind. He never spent one night there. Every time I came to this deserted place, I made myself at home by examining the huge stones on the walls inside and the outside walls as well. Who moved these big, heavy stones? Who picked out these stones that look like works of art?

Once, I wrote a little note on a piece of paper and stuck it in a tiny crevice between two rocks. I swore I'd never forget where I stashed that note. Nor would I forget what I had written. But to this day, I can't remember where it's hidden or the words I scribbled on it. At the time, I must have wanted someone, someday, to know I had made it that far.

Another time, I happened upon the deepest part of a valley. It was cool and shadowy, cluttered with fallen trees and nature composting in its own time. In that mossy place, I noticed a plain white wooden cross, three feet high. Apparently, someone had erected it on top of a raised mound, which appeared to be a grave. I scraped both knees climbing over huge fallen tree trunks and uprooted roots to get to the cross. I was determined to see what was inscribed on it.

When I reached the cross, I found no words on it at all. Not even a first name. Why would someone bother to come so deeply into these hills to mark a spot without any other remembrance? It remained a mystery to me, one that only the trees and the builder of that cross could unravel.

Another time – many times in fact – I found myself hiking far off in the deepest part of the woods when a mighty thunderstorm sprang up during the heavy heat of a late August afternoon. Usually, I was miles from the Abbey when the distant rumbling of thunder gave warning, and the trees branches began swaying like limbo dancers. These early signs let me know a terrific storm was on its way. Sometimes, I waited out the worst of it under the shelter of a group of protective pines.

Other times, though, when I realized I had to high-tail it back for Vespers and the last meal of the day, I pulled up my flimsy blue hood and raced back on slippery, red clay paths and leapt over rain-soaked rocks. By the time I made it back, I looked like the famed hermit monk who lives alone in the hills and only comes down once a year or so. Like him, I arrived soaked to the bone and covered in mud. Human-looking, but not quite.

One of my favorite discoveries, the place I ventured every year, was a little stream way, way back in the woods. Here, time and weather had worn away boulders thousands of years old to make them look like the surface of the moon. I teetered from one huge rock to another, following the creek as far down as I could. When I got to a patch of sun and a rock made for sitting, I pulled off my muddy running shoes and socks, dangling my hot, bare feet in the clean, cool water. The cold crept up my legs, to my heart, to the top of my head.

As I sat there cooling off, I listened to the quiet and thought about everything. Or nothing. Usually, I focused on what lay right in front of me instead of life in the real world, which, for these five short days, I gratefully left behind. Sitting alone there, listening to the whispering creek and insects jamming tunes with their wings, I always searched for one small rock to bring back home with me. To me, whichever rock I chose was a relic, a remembrance of being alone in a place where I felt at home. At peace. Maybe even loved.

Two years ago, though, my plan to be one with these sacred woods changed. Instead of bolting to the hills after breakfast, I went to the half-hour talk for retreatants. Not because I wanted to. I really didn't. I only went because my legs wouldn't let me explore the blue-green hills as they had in previous years.

Earlier that morning as the sun was baking away the sleepy fog, I crossed the two-lane highway to head down a stony path leading into the hills. Halfway down the path, though, my legs gave out. My double vision returned. I couldn't feel my feet. I stumbled to the side of the road, sank down beneath an old willow tree, and tried to pray. I couldn't find any words. All I heard was the beating of my heart.

After an hour or so, my legs regained some strength. I closed my right eye so I could see one path instead of two. I hobbled back to the Abbey with a walking stick I found in the woods. (When you need a walking stick out here, the perfect one always shows up within your reach. It never fails.) When I finally made it back to the monastery, I pulled myself by the hand railing up three flights of stairs to my room. When I got inside, I fell on my small bed with its gray blanket and wept.

This wasn't fair. This one part of my retreats I treasured most — being alone in the deep silent woods — was not to be mine this year. Maybe it would never be again. The thought paralyzed me.

Up in my room, choking back sobs so as not to disturb the silence of the others on the floor, I considered taking an early flight home from Louisville to New Hampshire. The agony of not being able to do what I always loved to do here seemed more than I could bear. Before finalizing an early departure, though, I went to the Guestmaster's talk that morning. To this day, I still don't know why.

Maybe I saw listening to someone else as a way of not dwelling, at least for a few minutes, on the joy I was missing out on in the solemn chaos of the Kentucky hills. The untouched wilderness where birds sang like angels. Where deer bounded freely across my path. Where winds whispered secrets meant only for me. Where I came closer to remembering the real me I had forgotten in the busyness of the real world (or as I've now come to see it, the unreal world).

Now, not knowing quite how I was supposed to spend these snail-paced minutes on this silent, unstructured retreat, I shuffled into the small conference room. I sat in the front row, off to the left, staring out the window. I watched a bright red cardinal bragging up to the sky. I followed a blue and yellow butterfly spiraling down and up until it found its place on a bush of slender purple stalks. A second butterfly joined in. Then a third. But watching this glory outside the window did little to raise my spirits. If anything, it reminded me of what I was missing in the deeper parts of this sacred place.

Before I could sink into terrific pity for myself, though, a white-haired monk the size of a linebacker walked into the room as quiet as a shadow. After introducing himself as Father Damien, he pulled up a stool in front of a dozen of us, lowered his head, crossed himself, and began with a simple prayer. "Father, we ask you to bless us during these five days. Help us listen to what it is You are saying to us through the silence in our hearts. Amen."

Then, without script or the practiced speech of an orator, Father Damien spoke about how little we humans grasp the magnificence of this world and our place – and divine purpose – in it. Sometimes, many times in fact, he stopped in mid-sentence (*"We think we're so important and in charge of everything, but . . ."*)

Then his marble-blue eyes stared up toward the window. He wasn't looking at the cardinal or the butterflies, though. He was looking at something none of us in this room could see. Something invisible but very real to him. In fact, during his frequent pauses, I felt as if he had left this room altogether and was visiting another dimension. Then, as if someone had tugged on his robe sleeve to remind him where he was, he turned back to us, grinned, and asked, "So, where was I?"

As Father Damien spoke, I listened. Carefully. I also studied his eyes. Sometimes, I stared so intensely at the blue light in his eyes that his words became background music to the image before me. But when he ended that first talk with these five simple words, "This is not your story," I heard every word loud and clear.

Those five words nearly broke my heart.

If this weren't my story, then whose was it? Who in her right mind could embrace a truth that wacky? A truth that proclaimed that Someone who supposedly loved you created a story in which you suffered? A story in which you found yourself in a pain-filled prison with no way out?

Others eagerly surrounded Father Damien after his talk to introduce themselves and ask him questions. I slipped out of the room, not totally grasping or totally agreeing with the "it's not my story" malarkey he had thrown out as if it were the most valuable treasure I could own. In my heart, the rocks I picked up in the woods seemed more precious to me than that crazy message he shared.

That year, even though I couldn't embrace every premise Father Damien offered, I went to all four of his talks. On the last day, he repeated his central message: We are not the authors of our lives. He also reminded us to be gentle on ourselves because the truth of Love lies beyond our grasp. We can come close to its meaning if we travel through life with open hearts. Few of us, though, choose that path, he admitted. We're too afraid to listen to our hearts. The world teaches us that if we live with our hearts wide open, we're in danger of being hurt. So we retreat to our place of control — the ideas that race around in our frantic minds — even though our own thoughts have never brought us one ounce of lasting peace.

If we really understood the immenseness of God's love, Father Damien added, our hearts would begin to soften so that we could embrace this invisible force. Then we would come to believe. And in that believing, we would greet each day with trust and gratitude no matter what we faced: emotional struggles, mental anguish, personal loss, tragic injustices, or life-altering physical pain and illness.

By the end of my retreat, my thoughts were scrambled even more than on that first day. My comfortable, preconceived notions had suddenly been morphed into an intricate web of sticky threads that kept tripping me up. More honestly, perhaps, I didn't want to let go of my own ideas and admit that I was not the sculptor of my own life. Such an admission sounded like a copout to me. A weakness of character where I gave up and gave in.

One thing I did grasp wholeheartedly, though: When Father Damien looked out beyond the windows into space with those pale blue eyes, he was directly connecting with the invisible power of Love. I may not have been able to bring Father Damien's words from my mind down into my heart yet.

But as to his true connection to Love? I had no doubt.

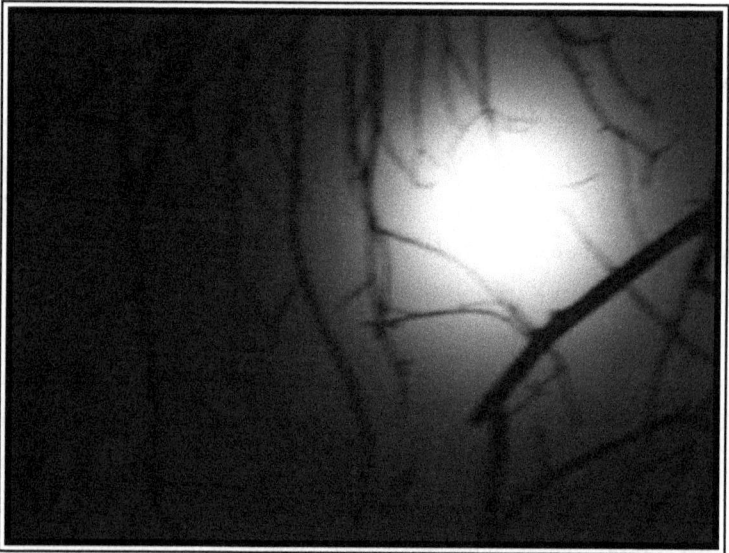

BUT I DON'T WANT TO WRITE ABOUT IT.

It was the last afternoon on the last day of the retreat. I never intended to stop by Father Damien's office to talk with him. A part of me wanted to — probably most of me did — but I didn't know what I would say once I got there.

Besides, every time I peeked toward his office on the first floor, a line of sojourners waited to talk with him. Who could blame them? He may not have given them the answers to their questions, but he leaned in and listened intently. And sometimes, you know, that's all we really want — someone to listen and hear the words we've been afraid to say out loud to ourselves let alone to anyone else.

But on that last day, when I glanced at his office on my way up to my room, no one was waiting. I stood outside his open door for one second.

"Hey, you. Come on in here."

Sheepishly, I smiled and shook my head. "I don't want to bother you. I just stopped by to say thank you. Your talks, they were great."

He smiled at me. "You're not bothering me. Come in. Sit down."

He pointed to a black chair by the door. His simple words hung between a command and an invitation. Either way, I knew I'd better sit.

"So, tell me about yourself," he began.

I leaned back in the chair. I hadn't come here to talk about myself. Not consciously, anyway. So I began with the easy stuff. The fluffy stuff on top of the layers. "Um, well, this is my seventh year coming to the Abbey. And I'm from New Hampshire."

"New Hampshire?" He sat back and smiled. "That's a long way from Kentucky. You know our order has a monastery in Massachusetts, don't you?"

"I know." I grinned. "But having to come this far and make plans four months in advance, it's like a pilgrimage for me. Plus, Thomas Merton and I share the same birthday. So of course I have to come to where he wrote and lived and to visit his grave."

Father Damien laughed. "Of course. Thomas Merton and you and the same birthday. That's the reason you travel hundreds of miles out of your way. But what else about you?"

"What else?"

"Yeah, like what do you do?"

Again, I played it safe with the parts of my life I could reel off at a cocktail party. "Well, I've taught college writing for twenty years. I write, too. And I have three grown children. They are amazing. My oldest, Emily, is getting her Ph.D. from Columbia, and my middle child, Joe, teaches down in the poorest part of Mississippi. My youngest one, Jeff, graduates from college this year. He always makes me laugh." I couldn't think of anything else to add.

"What about your husband?"

I blushed. This was not information I wanted to share. I cleared my throat. "Well, we were married for 25 years, but for the past five, we've been separated. It was a mutual decision. But mostly, it was mine. I felt as if things had changed. Or maybe I did. I don't know."

I looked down at my ringless fingers and held my breath. I prepared myself for the typical Catholic priestly advice of, "You know you need to keep working on your marriage because it's a sacrament."

But Father Damien didn't say that. He leaned forward and looked at me with those crystal blue eyes as if I might want to pay close attention to what he was about to say.

"Well then, it looks as if it's the time in your life to go forward. You've raised your children. You've worked on your marriage. Now this time is for you. To do what you need to do. To go where you need to go. So what would you like to do in this next chapter of your life?"

This conversation was getting a little deeper into my life than I had intended. But his asking was so genuine, I trusted him with real answers. "I did stop teaching and went to nursing school last year. It's something I thought I'd always want to do – care for people who were sick. I loved the classes and the other students. But then. . . ."

My voice broke.

"But then what?" His voice was gentle, his eyes kind.

"But then I got MS."

Saying these words out loud shocked me. It was the first time since learning I had MS eight months earlier that I had shared my diagnosis with anyone other than my immediate family and a few close friends. This wasn't something I wanted people to know. Call it pride. Or denial. Or fear. Or all three. You'd be right on all counts.

I expected Father Damien to say something like, "That is horrible." Or, "You poor thing." Or, at the very least, "I'm so sorry."

Instead, with his blue eyes blazing, he said, "That's amazing. Watching you this week, I would never have guessed anything was wrong with you. You seem so happy. You're always have a smile on your face."

I blinked back tears. "Really? I smile that much? Maybe I was born with a happy gene or something." I tried to laugh.

"So you have MS and you still look happy," he said. "Tell me about it. What's it like?"

I wasn't so sure I wanted to go into any great detail. It would make the MS sound too real. But Father Damien asked with the genuine concern of a child who doesn't know any better than to ask a question like that. Or maybe he does know better and that's why he asks. Because the childlike among us aren't nosy; they really want to feel what we're feeling. Still unshaped by the world, the innocent haven't lost the real part of themselves that connects to all of life. Soon, they'll forget. We all do. But for now, these pure souls still remember where they came from.

"I'd really like to know," Father continued, "because we had a Brother here who had MS. But he never talked about it. He also never smiled. But here you are, smiling. I'd really like to know your secret."

I inhaled and let the words tumble out: "I don't have any great secret. And as you can see from these tears I'm trying to hold back, I don't always smile or feel like jumping for joy. In fact, I almost didn't stay for the retreat this year."

"Because of the MS?"

I nodded. "The experience is so different for me this year. Before, I used to walk miles and miles into the woods. But now it feels as if some sadistic stranger broke inside my body and reprogrammed it so it doesn't work like it used to."

"How, exactly?"

I cleared my throat. "Well, people with MS have different symptoms. No two are alike. I used to sprint through these hills like a deer. Now, I'm lucky if I can make it up to my room on the third floor without tripping. My legs feel like cement blocks sometimes. Picture the Tin Man in the Wizard of Oz out in the rain without his oil can. He moves like a rusty robot. So do I."

He laughed. To my surprise, I did, too.

"But then at other times," I continued, "the legs go from being stiff to feeling like overcooked spaghetti noodles. Now I'm the Scarecrow without enough straw to fill up my legs. I go to take a step forward and without warning, one of my legs gives out, and I collapse to the ground."

He looked at me intently. Neither of us smiled.

I went on. "And then, too, I have this stupid double vision. So cross your eyes and imagine walking down the hall or looking at the pictures on your wall. You see two of everything. Which makes me dizzy, like the whole world is spinning around me. The doctors say the double vision usually only lasts a few weeks. But for me, it's been eight months now. I don't think I'll ever see one moon again."

He sat back in his chair. "So with all of this happening to you, what I still want to know is how you can be so happy."

My throat clogged up with a truth I had held in for too long. "Honestly, Father, I may look all right to you. And to everyone else. But that's because I'm faking it. I only walk far enough so no one sees me stumble. It's like I'm a music box. Once it runs out of energy, the music slows down to a complete stop until someone winds it up again. On the inside, I'm not at all happy about what's going on. In fact, I don't think I've ever been less happy."

He spoke gently. "God must have a lot in store for you to allow you to go through this."

I shot back. "But I don't want this. I want to be able to hike for miles in the woods again. To run like I used to. To see one moon at night instead of two. Maybe I should make up a sweatshirt that says, *"No, I'm not the Tin Man. No, I'm not the Scarecrow. And no, I'm not a drunk, either. I just have MS."*

"That's a good one," he said, smiling. "See? That's what I mean about keeping your sense of humor. You told me you're a teacher. And a writer. It would be a tremendous gift to others if you would write about your own journey with MS. You've helped me understand it better today. You could teach others, too."

I shook my head. "I don't want to write about it. I don't want to share this experience with anyone. I want to wake up one morning – yesterday would have been nice – and see that this has all been one bad dream."

"Then write about those feelings, too. It's part of the process."

"The process of this story that isn't mine, right?"

"So you were listening to my talks." He grinned.

"I heard every word. And I know that what you're saying about me not being in control is most likely the truth. But it's hard to be off-the-wall joyful about that idea right now. I don't even know myself how I feel other than being petrified of the future while looking back over my shoulder and thinking the best parts of my life are over."

Father Damien clasped his mighty hands together and leaned toward me. "I understand this might be hard for you to write about. But I, for one, would really like to know more about what you're going through. Where this challenge leads you. Everyone has something to deal with in life. What you write might help them cope. I'd read your book about your journey."

I laughed as he walked me to the door. "Well, at least I know I have one book sold."

"Yep. Now all you have to do is write it. Actually, just wait and let the real Author take over. See what happens."

"Maybe someday I will," I said.

He winked at me before he went down the stairs to the church. "You will, someday."

I half-smiled at him.

But between you and me, that someday seemed about as far away as that little creek deep in the woods where one special rock would not be mine to take home this year.

OK, THEN –
YOU WRITE IT.

I had more than an hour before Vespers, so I went up to my room to lie down and rest. My racing mind, though, wouldn't settle down. So I got up, grabbed my green suede journal, and shuffled down three flights of stairs and out to a bench beneath a maple tree in front of the Abbey. For the first time in eight months, I took out my pencil and began scribbling every thought that came to me. For an hour, my pencil kept moving. I didn't erase or edit anything. Nor did I bother to read this entry again. Not until now.

August 20, 2009. Tuesday. 4:00 p.m. or close to it.

So this is not my story, huh? I may star in it. But it's not mine. It's the Author's.

And I can prove it.

Ask me when my story first began. I can't say for certain.

Ask me how and when it will end. I don't know one thing about that.

Except like all stories on earth — yours, too — it will end. Someday. Before it begins again at the beginning.

But when and how that will happen, I couldn't begin to say.

Oh, I can imagine and wish how I'd like my story to go. But my imagining and wishing still don't make me the Real Author. The Real Author is the one who sees the big picture. The front side of the tapestry. It's already been created.

I don't know how. Or why.

Why would my measly little life here on earth cause anyone to sculpt a whole book around it? Today, I'm feeling about as plain and lonesome as that little quivering leaf hanging among thousands on the branch above me.

There's nothing special about that leaf. Nothing special about me, either.

I hear my Author laugh.

"But you are the star of one of my best-sellers!"

Now it's my turn to laugh. Better yet, to complain.

"Oh, really? Well if that's true, couldn't you have made me a real star then, one that lights up the sky instead of a star that tumbles out of its constellation and drops down into the woods? Or how about making me a singing cardinal instead of a cawing crow? Or giving me a body that moves like a gazelle instead of an old jalopy that burns out and ends up in some junkyard?"

The Real Author stays silent.

So do I.

A warm wind blows. I watch white clouds drift across a hazy blue sky. I wish it would rain. Not a little drizzle. Or even a startling cloudburst. But a mighty storm full of fury and fierceness, relentless thunder and hot, fiery lightning. Bolts that begin thirty thousand feet above my head and strike down to the ground, electrifying everything in sight.

I want a storm like that to transform everything down here. I want it to transform me.

"OK," my Guide says after listening to my silent thoughts. "Here's the pen. You write your story as you'd like it to be."

I quickly reach with my left hand to grab the pen. Just as quickly, I pull it back. "No. I'd mess everything up if I were in charge."

The One Who Knows holds out the pen again and says, "You said you want to write it. I understand. You really can write it if you choose."

I shake my head. "No. You're like the genie giving me three wishes. What I think I want would only make my life worse in the long run."

My Author sits down next to me.

I want to cry. She sees those inside tears I'm trying to hide. She knows everything. My life is the Author's story to tell, a story she knew before I was even born. I dare to turn and look into Her eyes and I see: She is crying, too. Because I am.

Because I am? My Author cares that much?

Why?

If He really did care, wouldn't my story be full of joy and happiness and laughter — and love? Wouldn't I be whole and healthy instead of weak and wobbly?

My Author reads my heart and moves closer.

"So far in my story for you, haven't you not once but an infinite amount of times known my gifts of joy, happiness, laughter, and love?"

I think back, not to where the story began. I don't remember that moment. But as for the chapters that followed, many of those I can recall.

I remember chapters with playgrounds and red wooden swings and trees made for hiding. I remember double rainbows and double scoops of fudge ripple ice cream cones. I remember lightning bugs dancing before my eyes like stars and lightning streaking through the sky like tree branches on fire. I remember the joy of playing the piano and how my childhood friends laughed at my Wizard of Oz imitations and said my version of the cowardly lion's song was better than the original.

I remember canoeing up a river where I could see every rock on the bottom, and I remember leaning back in that silver canoe and letting the current carry me back to the dock. I remember summer months of bare feet, river baths, exploring untamed hills, and discovering one secret path speckled with real West Virginia glass stones. All of these chapters brought me enormous happiness. I remember.

Watching clouds. Waiting for a falling star. Feeling my heart pound and my cheeks flush with fire over my first crush. Climbing a favorite tree. Laughing until I couldn't breathe. Learning to jump rope and ride a bike and hula hoop and do a flip off the diving board when I turned forty.

Listening to Beethoven's sonatas cracking out from my father's radio late at night when I was ten and hearing a train whistle from the other side of town. Wondering about where that train was headed and whether or not anyone else in the house heard the syncopated rhythms between Beethoven's music and that distant train.

I remember going back to sleep, rocked safely by those sounds, without the fear of having that same nightmare where I tried to fly but couldn't.

Yes, I remember all those little things. Insignificant to others but vital to me. And I remember my greatest gifts of all — gifts I could never have imagined or created myself, my three children: Emily. Joe. And Jeff. And oh, so many others. People that came into my life for a period. Or a paragraph. Or for the better part of my story.

"You are right," I admit. "I have known more happiness in my life than any one person deserves. It's just so hard now because I remember how I used to feel whole and healthy and happy. But now. . .

The Author already knows my next thought.

Maybe when I felt healthy and whole two years ago, I really wasn't all that happy. Not deep inside, anyway. Maybe I was just going about the busyness of life. Being an important college professor. Being a well-known *writer for our local paper. Being engaged in my children's lives and the things that made them happy.*

Maybe in all that doing, I didn't know real happiness for myself. Or true unconditional love. I certainly loved my children and had a real passion for my teaching. But as for loving myself and being grateful every second for my life in a deep, real way? Suddenly, I'm not so sure about that. Maybe all that doing actually prevented me from being more open to love, from taking greater risks, from having the humility to listen. From having the courage to change.

I'm not sure about then. But I do know about now.

And now this part of my life seems too crammed with sadness for happiness to enter into it. As far back as I can remember, this is the hardest time I've ever known.

"*I've known many chapters that contained happiness. But if you don't mind,*" *I plead to this Spirit,* "*could you please take this MS away so I can know happiness in a new, real way? I promise I'll be more grateful this time around.*"

My Love pulls me close. Like a child grateful for a parent's lap, I don't resist. Right now, I'm too tired to struggle. Too tired of trying to figure out my place in this story. Too tired to ask, beg, or make any more bargains.

"Lorraine," My Author's breath gently brushes my neck, "the place where you are now – this part of the story – it's not a whole chapter. Not even one full page. Maybe it's not even a word."

"*This hard time isn't even a word? What else, if not words, make up a story?*"

The Spirit laughs.

"*I don't see what's so funny,*" *I grumble.* "*After all, I am the one going through this sad story you supposedly wrote out of love for me.*"

"You're not going through the story," My Author explains. "You <u>are</u> the story."

"Now I really don't get it." I roll my eyes.

"Take a breath and think. In addition to words, what else do you need so that the whole writing makes sense to a reader?"

I stop and look at these charcoaled scribbles on these pages. I don't know. What else does a writer need besides words in order for the meaning to be clear?

I pause. I frown. I stare at this page again. And again. As a so-called writer, I should know this. After a few more minutes, I slowly begin to see.

"Two things!" I say with the joy of a child who has just found the last remaining objects in a scavenger hunt.

"Go on." My Author smiles.

"For one thing, a writer needs punctuation marks to show endings and pauses. Marks to distinguish between essential and nonessential thoughts. Marks to make necessary separations as well as marks to show connections. And then those final marks that reveal questions, answers, and astonishment."

My Author beams at me like a parent watching a baby take her first steps on her own.

"Wonderful! But two things you said. What is the other?"

I grin with pride because I know this answer is right, too. "A writer needs spaces. Otherwise, letters fall into letters, words into words, shifting points into shifting points. Who could figure out what the writer has to say if the writer ignores the spaces?"

I scribble out sentences crashing into one another in order to prove my point:

"Itwouldlooksomethinglikethisandwhoshouldhavetoworkthathar dinordertoseewhatwouldotherwisebeclearitwouldlooklikechaositwould

*bechaosandconfusioninplaceofasimpletruththatmayhelpsomeonewhensh
eneedsitthemost."*

"Aha!" My Teacher beams at me again. "And what about that space? What exactly do you think it is?"

Another puzzler. What is space? Maybe it's like air. Or gravity. A force you know is there but you can't see it or hold it in your hands. But you know it's real because you can breathe. Plus, you're not floating off the pavement like a helium balloon.

"Space is really nothing." *I shrug.*

"Exactly!" My Author hugs me.

"Exactly? Exactly what?"

"Nothing is something!" My Author claps her hands with delight as if nothing is the answer to everything.

I still don't understand, but it's all right. Right now, I feel content in not knowing what She means. She stands up and we begin to walk together in silence. I stop worrying about who or where I am in the story. Whether I'm in a word, a pause, or any empty space, it doesn't matter. I sense that wherever I am, I'm being taken care of. For this moment anyway, which, I realize, is all I have. It's all we ever have.

I closed my journal and headed back to the Abbey. I walked slowly, one foot in front of the other, looking three feet in front of me. A strong, warm breeze mussed my already messy hair. A bird called out, "Tweet, tweet, tweet." Or was it saying, "Sweet, sweet, sweet"?

The branches in the pine trees sighed as a stronger gust of wind blew its way through them. The whooshing through the pines sounded like the wind and the tree had conspired to sing out one word for me: "Exactly."

Exactly. This was not my story. That was exactly as it was supposed to be.

Along the stone walkway, I composed a silent prayer:

Forgive me whoever you are
For not believing
That this is Your story
Written out of love for me.
Let it unfold as You will.
Send down Your grace, like rain,
To soak my dying roots. Help me
make Your dream of me come true.

As the final bell chimed to signal the beginning of Vespers, I stopped on the top step before entering the church. I turned around to watch heavy clouds racing through the blue-grey sky. Tonight, I knew for certain, that storm I wished for this morning would arrive in all its power and glory.

True to the story the clouds foretold, a mighty thunderstorm descended into these Kentucky hills after Compline, the prayer that signals the ending of the day. That night, I scooted my little bed close to the two tall windows that face the mountains. I raised the blinds all the way up so that I could have a front row seat to this spectacular drama that performed throughout most of the night. There was so much lightning, so much fire, I felt as if I were looking into the sun.

I closed my eyes. I had to. But even with eyes closed, I still saw and felt the light. At some point during the storm, I drifted off to sleep.

A few minutes after 8:00 that next morning, Father Damien poked his head into my room. My faded blue suitcase still lay open, half-empty on the bed.

"I see you're still here," he said.

"Yes, I'm sorry. I'm always the last one when it comes to leaving."

He waited patiently in the hallway while I tossed the rest of my dirty clothes into my suitcase. I took one last look out the windows. The storm that passed in the night left clouds, white and pink, floating in an ocean blue sky. I could stay here forever.

"The time here always starts out so slow and then like a snowball, it ends up going way too fast," I said to Father Damien.

He smiled at me. "The world has things for you to do."

"Like write that book?"

"I hope you do," he said.

"Well, guess what? I already have the title. It came to me last night during the storm. Actually, it's a title you gave me: *This Is Not My Story.*"

He clapped his hands together and grinned. "Perfect. So now all you have to do is go and write it."

"I will. I promise," I said.

It would take me another eighteen months, though, before I began to make good on that promise.

HEY, BUDDY, I REALLY DON'T LIKE THE WAY YOUR STORY IS GOING.

The reason I delayed writing this book was not that I didn't feel a greater peace coming back into the world from the Abbey. I did. Over the years, I've learned that the peace from those five days somehow lasts until, down to my very last drop of grace, I drive down that hidden country Kentucky road at the end of which the stone wall leading to the Abbey appears. I see the red light blinking at the entrance. I slow down. I breathe deeply. I'm back home again.

I also didn't delay writing this because I doubted Father Damien's five words, "This is not your story."

The fact is, I did start writing it. The day I got home. I heard that first line – "This is not a book I want to write" – but then I stopped. I knew that opening line, which came from Someone else through me, worked well. It was, as they say in writer's lingo, a "grabber."

But then, once the world came back into my life — or rather once I chose to ground both feet firmly into the world's muck — I realized the truth of that first line: I really did not want to write this book. At least not the way my Author was unfolding it in front of me.

I felt physically stronger at the Abbey, but soon after I came home, my vision worsened. My legs turned into either stone columns or overcooked pasta. I picked up a urinary tract infection, which isn't uncommon with MS. I also got a sinus infection. My fever spiked off and on for weeks, which made me dizzy and caused my heart to pound like a jackhammer. Some days, I doubted whether I could make it down my fifty-foot driveway to the mailbox. I somehow always managed to make it there, but too often for my liking I had to stop three or four times before reaching my own back door. This lack of control over my legs did not fill me with any great joy, let me tell you.

Still, I kept reminding myself of the truth I longed to bring down from my mind into my heart: that every part of my story was written for my own good. But I wanted my own say in this matter, too. That ego, you know, is a powerful force. The weaker we become, the more it breaks down the front door and takes over as the head of our household.

And take over it did.

Collapsing on the couch for the third time one morning, my monstrous ego and I had this brilliant idea that even though Someone else was the director of my life, we could ask that Someone to make room for us in the editing booth. We, then, could be the co-authors. As co-authors, this story would be a cooperative effort with my will being as important as the Original Author's.

So here's what my ego and I suggested to the Writer of my story:

"How about if we create me, Your main star, as coming back from that holy place, the Abbey, and suddenly I can walk again like I used to. That sounds rather spectacular if you ask me. (Not that Anyone asked.) Not only that, but how about if You and I surprise the reader with this uplifting twist: My legs are so strong and my vision so straight that I can now run farther than ever before.

"My doctors remain mystified. No one has ever spiraled up the MS ladder like this. Being tenacious and disciplined, this odds-defying woman, me, then signs up for the Boston Marathon. Since the farthest I've run is three miles, naturally I don't win that race. We can't be too unrealistic here or our readers won't believe a word of this story.

"But in the haze of the early evening, exhausted and hobbling like a wounded soldier, I finally cross the finish line. There my three children wait for me with tears and cheers. They all hug me and say, 'Mom, we never thought you could do it, but you did it!'

"Then I humbly kneel – or collapse if You'd prefer – onto the hard pavement. Once I have the strength to speak, I announce the real truth: 'No, it wasn't I who made it. It was the Almighty Source who wrote this chapter into my story. I only chose to run the race, to overcome my fear, so that I could announce the glory of this Great Author.'

"And in my proclamation, the first star of the evening appears. Venus, the goddess of love, blazes in the heavens while a choir of angels sings out with such glory on high that the whole population of Boston hears about my miraculous run. People near and far, even the greatest of cynics, open wide the windows of their hearts and come to believe in a power greater than themselves. And that power is Love."

In my mind, as the plot continues, the Almighty, whom I have now designated as my assistant-in-training, says, "Wow, this is a terrific story! I'll write it exactly as you've suggested. With your approval, I'll also add more details to keep the reader intrigued. Because as a writer you know that showing is so much more effective than telling. So let's get started by putting you in your running shoes at the starting line. What color would you like them to be? Purple or orange? Yellow and pink polka dots, perhaps?"

But um, apparently the Main Author wasn't so keen on me being in the commander's seat and rewriting the story quite this way. And why should She be? In truth, I wasn't asking to be the co-author; I was shoving Her aside and telling my underling the way I wanted my story to go.

From the messages I heard at the Abbey, the point in trusting that Someone else was writing my story was not to tell that Someone what words to write but rather to listen to the words I was given. To submit to that which was not within my control.

This idea sounded doable in the quiet lights of the church. But back in the glare of the world, I was having a hard time embracing the truth that this story wasn't mine to write at all. It was only mine to trust. My ego refused to give up its power. My heart and soul, though, tried to hold on to this truth: "Being submissive is not a sign of weakness. It's a sign of faith in Something greater, wiser, and more loving than I." Or so I kept telling myself.

Then, too, even if we are the world's greatest doubters, the firmest non-believers in anything other than this temporal world, our logical selves confirm the premise that we are not in 100 percent control of our destinies. Even if we can't grasp this idea on a spiritual level, on a scientific level we see the lack of control in our lives every day.

Think about it. In this world, who or what listens to our commands? The weather or which way the winds blow? No. We certainly can't control into which family we're born or where we are raised, either. Given any other ancestry ladder, I could be the Queen of England. A Scottish bartender named James. Or a starving child in Ethiopia who has only minutes left to live.

To quote the great scientist and writer Lewis Thomas, "Statistically, the probability of any one of us being here is so small that you'd think the mere fact of existing would keep us all in a contented dazzlement of surprise."

Dazzlement is a gift given to us humans, the only living creatures on this earth who can realize our own existence (as far as we know). We can thank our spiritual selves as well as our genetic makeup for this self-awareness. Did you realize that human beings and pumpkins share 93 percent of the same genes? A little give and take on the genome ladder, and we could be enjoying one season of glory in Farmer Brown's vegetable field. (Maybe pumpkins, too, feel dazzled out there in the warm September sunlight. But given what we know, it's not their conscious choice to feel that way.)

In fact according to geniuses among us, of all the four forces that control our lives – our desires, the environment, fate, and genes – it is our genes and not our own plans that play the most dominant role.

As humans, though, we like to believe – we are taught to believe – that what we want is the most powerful force controlling not only ourselves but everything and everyone around us. You know the modern sayings: "If you dream it, you can be it." Or "Wish hard enough and all your dreams will come true."

The idea of individuals wanting power and control in their lives is not confined to our modern era. Think of the Adam and Eve story. Or of Icarus. But the idea of individuals being the source of their own power really took off in the enticing Western psychology of the 1960s. And we all (at least most of us) bought into it. Power is an alluring force, a siren calling out to the seasick sailors alone at sea. Listen to the song of your ego, and you will see how it tries to direct your every step and thought.

Admittedly, in some cases, yes, we can achieve the goals we set out for ourselves. But what about the young man who dreams to be a pilot and loses his eyesight? What about the woman who trained to be a concert pianist but whose right hand is severely damaged in a car accident? What about the student who wants to be a surgeon but was born with Down Syndrome? Wish as hard as these three might, the dreams that they've set up for themselves can't come true.

However, that doesn't mean their stories have unhappy endings. On the contrary. That blind man may choose instead to help himself and others fly with their own inner wings by becoming a musician or a writer. When her dreams to play the piano fail, that woman may choose to switch dreams and discover a cure for cancer. The child with Down Syndrome may not be able to heal others physically, but she can heal our doubts about the real meaning of life through her examples of trust and unconditional love.

Although we can't control so many factors in our lives, the one thing we can control – the single most important gift humans alone receive – is the gift of choosing our perspective on life.

I attribute this powerful notion on perspective to my dear friend, Roger Croteau, artist, psychologist, and priest. As he has said to me on more than one occasion, "When you change your level of awareness, Lorraine, you begin to attract a new reality."

The following metaphor from the Kamir adds to the understanding of Father Croteau's wisdom:

"All see that the drop merges into the ocean,

But few see that the ocean merges into the drop."

In other words, we can either view our life circumstances (the ocean) as swallowing up our tiny, insignificant selves. Or we can look at life (the ocean) as filling us up and making us greater than we could ever imagine. In the end, realizing we have the choice to change how we view our lives makes all the difference as to whether we walk looking down at the ground or lift our eyes to see what exists beyond the mountaintops.

If we choose to look up and perceive life as a chance to celebrate our stories, which have been given to us out of love, then how can we not see joy and love within and around us? How can we not wake up and be thankful for this day we have been given? For did we create this day? We did not. And could this day be our last? Yes, it could. It could also, according to Our Artist, be our first.

On the other hand, if we choose to believe we are ultimately in control, then what happens when those "best laid plans of mice and men" fail despite our best efforts? How do we handle our lives then? If we are the ones in charge, then how can we not help but feel like failures when our plans don't work out? How can we not fall into depression or be paralyzed by anxiety when we don't live up to our own or to others' expectations? How can we not feel as if our lives are nothing but the roll of the dice in a Reno casino, and when those dots don't add up as we wish them to, we are nothing but losers?

From the negative perspective I had chosen, struggling with my own erratic steps made me feel as if the entire deck had been stacked against me. I used to be a runner. But now, here I was: one wobbly step forward, then three rigid steps back. Then once too often, boom, boom, boom, face down on the side of the road in the darkness with an aching right elbow, a bruised knee, and shattered sense of pride.

OK, since I promised to be honest in this book, I'm going to write something I'd rather not admit. After coming off of this wonderful retreat and the truths I heard at the Abbey, I still found myself reaching out to control the reins. The next month when instead of being miraculously healed I actually got worse, that Author of my story was far from my best buddy.

That's putting it mildly.

With every missed step, I felt forgotten. Betrayed. Like a child left in a basket on a stranger's doorstep, I felt abandoned and unloved. And angry. Why did I ever buy into that illogical notion that Someone out there loved me and that the worsening of my MS symptoms was for a greater purpose? I was also fuming at that Someone who seemingly left me stranded on this dark path without a lantern to light my way.

Why? What had I done wrong?

Was it that my faith wasn't strong enough? Was it that I had failed as a wife? Was it that I didn't think of or give thanks to my Creator often enough? Meister Eckhart, a 13th century monk, once said that two words alone make up the perfect prayer: "Thank you." After reading this quote years ago, I always aimed to say thank you whenever I thought of it. Did my Author know, though, that I often gave thanks to see if I could talk Him into inserting an easier chapter into my story? That my "thank you's" actually served as my bargaining tools?

As any author knows, before you can write a good story, you have to know your main character inside and out. Everything from the number of hairs on her head to the dark chambers in his heart. Maybe the Author had had enough of my moaning. Enough of my stubborn will. Enough of my childish bargaining. Enough of my vapid words without a heart beating behind them.

Despite whining on this lonely road, though, I did not totally stop believing that Someone was out there somewhere. (Yes, I know after what I wrote about our own dreams being the last factor to influence us, this may seem like a paradox – that I still believed. But I did. What can I say? If you asked me to list my three favorite songs, they'd be "Somewhere over the Rainbow," "An Impossible Dream," and "Climb Every Mountain.")

In a way, I had no choice but to believe. If I were going to get out of bed everyday, I had to hold on to the hope that a Loving Spirit walked with me even though I couldn't see or feel anything. I give much credit to my upbringing for these last remaining embers of faith. Since early in my childhood, I have not only had a deep faith in my Creator, but this faith had been actualized more than once.

Here's one such story:

One Saturday afternoon, Illinois snowdrifts came up to my ten-year old waist while the bitter cold wind turned my cheeks into red apples with white centers. Being Catholic, and since I had been sick and missed confession with my fourth grade class on Friday, I had to admit to lying, disobeying my parents, and fighting with my brothers and sisters on a Saturday in order to receive Holy Communion at Sunday Mass.

(Until seventh grade, these three sins made up my standard response for every confession. Once I reached seventh grade, though, I had to add swearing and "unclean thoughts" to the list. Wishing for Dennis Cosgrove to hold my hand and kiss me didn't seem all that impure to me. But since that phrase was in the Catechism, so I had to include it. Keep in mind this was 1962, six years before the Second Vatican Council began to replace the burdens of guilt and sin with the gifts of acceptance and love.)

Since my two brothers and two of my sisters had already made their confessions on Friday, I had to journey nine blocks to the church and back alone. From the first step out the back door, tremendous loneliness engulfed me. The five of us always made this trip together. We threw snowballs at each other. Played tag. In the springtime, we cut through neighbors' back yards and made private, well-packed trails of mud through their flowerbeds. The more mud, the better.

On this winter day, though, the sun was already casting red streaks into a gray-metal sky. It was just me out there, trudging along through white-blue snow. I don't even remember any cars passing by on Stephenson Avenue. Like the inside of me, the streets were empty, too. I thought about not going to confession at all. Who would know? I could say I went and show up back home an hour later.

But that Catholic guilt thing wouldn't let me add a fourth lie to the three I had memorized for the week. So like it or not, the church was the only place where I could thaw out. I finally made it to St. Thomas Aquinas Church and pulled open the heavy wooden door. A line of older parishioners had already filled the right aisle to the confessional from the front to the back of the church. I stood at the end, feeling sorrier and sorrier for myself. My toes were numb; my cheeks stung. Given the fact that old people's sins were bigger than mine since they had had more time to sin, this would take forever. Which meant that by the time my turn came, the red streaks in the sky would loom as gray scars and the journey back home darker and icier than ever.

Since I was one of the last penitents in line, Father O'Neil gave me a light sentence. I think he was savoring the thought of his prime rib dinner back at the rectory. "Say three Hail Mary's, and go in peace," he said. That was it.

I knelt down in the back pew on the wooden kneeler, unexpectedly at ease with being in this warm place where the red tabernacle light remained constant. I sat back in the pew after I quickly said my three prayers, closed my eyes, and breathed in the smell of incense and varnish.

The overhead lights went out, meaning Father had already left the church through the back door. So it was just me, in this quiet place, with that one glowing red light. In this one brief moment, everything in my world seemed all right. I could even feel my toes again.

But I knew I couldn't stay much longer in this sanctuary. My stomach grumbled, and the cold on the way back would dip down into the tiny bones of my fingers and toes the longer I waited. Sooner, rather than later, I had to leave.

An amazing thing happened, though. Once I shoved open the heavy wooden door, the outside world felt like the first day of summer. I stood on that top step feeling more love, more joy than I had ever known before. Was it because I had been to confession? I don't think so. I had admitted to these same three sins every week for two years and had never felt such lightness of heart before.

Instead of hurrying home, I took my time. I noticed the lights coming through my neighbors' steamed-up kitchen windows. I listened to my own breathing and marveled as my exhales formed little cloud puffs in the air. I delighted in the ice-covered snow as it crunched beneath my boots and delighted even more when I could glide over a frozen patch without cracking the ice. I forgot about my frozen toes and looked up to witness the first star of the evening curtsy in the sky. I would have made a wish, but I couldn't think of anything I would wish for.

As I made my way back home, I couldn't explain it, but I knew: I was walking in the presence of Something I had never felt before. And that Something proved to me that I was now, was then, and would always be loved beyond a love I could ever imagine.

Which is to say that now, even though I often felt forsaken on this journey with MS, I knew this wasn't true. Something buried deep in my soul refused to let me forget that cold winter day when one flickering red flame won out over the darkness.

Forty-some years later, I still tried to believe that Love lived somewhere within me. Even when I bumbled up steps to my freshmen writing classes. Even when I stumbled down those three flights, too. When I saw thirty-six students before me instead of eighteen. When I wrote on the board with my left hand only to have the chalk shatter on the floor because my fingers went numb. When I snapped an elastic purple patch over one eye so I could drive home without seeing two of everything speeding toward me.

Even then, I tried to believe. But one starless night while I was out walking, my legs gave out. I fell on both knees and ended up in the road. Struggling to regain the strength to stand up, I lifted my head off of the ground and yelled out, "Hey Buddy, I really don't like the way Your story is going. Could you do me a big, fat favor and change it?"

In reply, I heard nothing but silence.

THE ANSWER YOU SEEK
IS SIMPLE, MY DEAR.

Years ago, I heard this story about a woman who lost her only child and what she had to do in order to go on with her life despite her overwhelming grief:

After two-years of struggling in constant pain, the mother travels to a distant mountaintop to consult a well-known hermit who is said to know the answers to life's greatest challenges. All the way along her journey, the woman weeps tears as big as pebbles. She can barely see the path beneath her feet. One more day of such heartache, and she fears that the only way to end her pain is to veer off the path toward the cliff and end her own life.

Finally, though, she reaches the top of the mountain where she hears the old hermit humming in his cave. With tears still streaming down her face, she falls on her knees and begs, "Please come out, old man. Two years ago, I lost my only child. She was the most precious gift in the world to me. My source of joy. My everyday light. But since the morning she died, I have not been able to find a way to stop these tears or think about anything but this bleeding in my heart. Please help me find a way to go on with my life again or else I, too, must die."

Bent over like a young birch in winter, the humming hermit shuffles out of his cave. Slowly, he kneels down beside the woman and smiles at her with great tenderness.

"The answer you seek is simple, my dear. In fact, it is right around the corner from where you live. Rest here awhile but then return to your village. There you will find another mother who has lost her only two children. Go over and visit with this woman. In sharing her pain, your own grief will lessen until the tears you cry turn into pearls of joy."

The moral of the old hermit's story is clear: Reaching out to someone whose suffering is worse than ours eases our own pain and helps us move forward in our lives.

Before my diagnosis of MS, this parable made sense to me. Compassion for others contained the key to living a good and happy life. In connecting with others, our own sense of disconnection, the true source of all suffering, disappeared. Before the MS, it was easy for me to put suffering in perspective. The suffering of others, that is.

"You think your life is tough because you can't eat steak any time you like? What about the starving children in Africa, 100 of whom will die in this hour because they don't have a tablespoon of rice?"

"You can't afford to go to that Ivy League college because you don't have enough money? What about the 70 percent of kids in the Mississippi Delta who won't graduate from high school this year because no one cares enough to educate them?"

"Oh, so your basement flooded again this spring? Well, at least you have a home. What happens to the homeless when the weather drops so low their bones turn to ice?"

Before my own suffering, it was so easy to reel off these words of wisdom: No matter what the circumstances, someone has it better than we do and someone has it much worse. It may not be fair, but, echoing the Sinatra song, "That's life."

As I said, before my diagnosis I quickly embraced this concept on a practical level. I could even feel its truth tugging at my heart and keeping it open to the suffering of others. Being a person of compassion was who I always was. Or, rather, who I thought I was.

But now that it was my turn to journey on an unpredictable course, I found that comparing my circumstances to those of others didn't help. Instead of aiming to connect with the suffering of others, I was totally focused on myself, constantly bargaining with God to "please, please, please make me like I used to be."

Being so angry with my physical changes and the fear of the future, a huge part of my heart clenched up like a fist. It not only shut out my Creator, who obviously wasn't answering my requests (at least not as far as I could see), but it also closed my heart to the hardships of others.

For example, from my youngest sister's firsthand experience in a hospital outside of Baghdad, I had seen the pictures of innocent children burned to death. I had seen the faces of the mothers as they wept at the sky. I had heard her stories of unimaginable cruelties to innocent Iraqi civilians as well as the traumas, external and internal, that afflicted our American soldiers.

Even closer to home, many of my friends were bearing crosses far heavier than my own. My friend Ginger was battling ovarian cancer for the fourth time. My friend Leile lost her older son when he fell off a dormitory roof his sophomore year in college. And then there was my friend, JoAnn. She was diagnosed with MS ten years earlier and now struggled with the simplest tasks, like making it to the bathroom on time or driving a car.

JoAnn, the wife of one of my husband's co-workers, had once been a dancer. A really, really good dancer. She performed in plays and in troupes, and nothing made her feel so joyful as when she moved her body like a daisy in the wind. In her heart, JoAnn was a dancer, and next to her husband, John, and young daughter, Annie, dance was her greatest love.

Then one day ten years ago, JoAnn was rehearsing for a play. She missed a step. She tripped. She laughed it off as being too tired. But when the next rehearsal came, instead of lifting her legs like strong tree limbs, she could barely get her toes off the floor.

One month later, she was diagnosed with MS. No one could believe it. How could such a horrible disease attack this beautiful, forty-two-year old woman who lived to make others smile through her gift of dance and her love for others?

Every time I saw JoAnn at a company function, it was clear how quickly her disease was progressing. First, she would walk slowly, holding on to John's arm. The next time we'd meet up, she would hold his arm and balance herself with a cane. Later, John had to help her go to the ladies room, holding her arm like an exquisite porcelain doll. A doll who kept a smile on her ashen face even though she had to ask for her husband's help to go to the bathroom.

Soon after that, JoAnn didn't attend any company functions. "It's too hard for her to go out," John explained. "She has a walker now. That makes it easier for her to get around the house. But getting in and out of cars is too much for her."

All the rest of us would offer our sympathy and tell him to give JoAnn our best. Then we would order another round of drinks and switch the subject. "You really should call JoAnn," my husband, from whom I had been separated for five years, advised me after I told him about my diagnosis. "She might be able to help you with this."

I had already been thinking of JoAnn nonstop whenever my own legs wouldn't take me as far as they used to. But whenever I went to dial her number, I was overcome with fear. And a tidal wave of guilt.

If I really were JoAnn's friend, I should have called her long ago to see how she was doing. To see if I could do anything for her. To keep her company or to take her out. But at that time, I was healthy and fine and going about my own insulated life, teaching and writing and raising my three children. Whenever I thought of JoAnn during the time I could still run three miles every morning and walk another three miles each night, I didn't just pray for her healing. I also thanked God for keeping me so healthy. For allowing my legs to be so strong.

It isn't easy for me to reveal this self-absorbed part of myself. In fact, I am ashamed realizing how selfish and insensitive I was. But looking honestly at this dark chamber within my heart, when I thought about JoAnn, the truth is, I thanked God I didn't have this disease.

Then one beautiful May morning nearly four years ago, I caught the toe of my shoe on a curb while I was running across a four-lane highway in Cleveland, Mississippi. I crashed down like an oak tree uprooted by a tornado. "I just ran too far," I consoled myself as I hobbled up to my motel room to clean the blood off of my knees and elbows.

Two months later, I tumbled down the front bank while I was mowing the lawn. I banged my forehead on the ground, luckily missing a huge boulder inches away from me. I jumped up as fast as I could, mainly because I didn't want the neighbors to see my face and hair plastered with mud. This time I reasoned, "I should have done this part of the yard first when I wasn't so tired."

Two weeks later, I couldn't feel the big toe on my right foot. "It must be something pressing on a nerve," I deduced. "Probably something went out of whack when I fell down the bank."

In the middle of August, three days before my scheduled hike to the west coast of Scotland, my first adventure alone in a foreign country, the backs of my legs started to tighten up. I felt a strange numbness in my lower back. I also felt a strange numbness on my right calf, as if I were wearing a woolen knee sock.

Still, I thought whatever was happening with my body had to do with pressure on some nerve. I was a little anxious about going on such a new adventure to my grandfather's homeland when I didn't feel completely like myself. But I figured that when I got back from my eight-day hike, I would go see my chiropractor and an orthopedic doctor and get whatever was causing the numbness straightened out.

That was early September 2007. I had stopped teaching in order to take nursing classes, something I had always wanted to do. Besides being interested in medicine, having a career in the medical field would assure me of financial independence when and if my husband and I parted ways for good. Plus, like teaching, nursing was a direct way to help others. It was, I thought, my second calling.

During my Anatomy and Physiology courses, I devoured every word in my textbooks. I wrote down everything my professor said. I made hundreds of note cards. I memorized every chart, every hormonal pathway. From what I learned in my nursing books, I was still convinced that that these physical changes had to do with some trauma to my back. From falling or running. Or something.

An MRI of my lumbar region would show that pressed nerve in my back. I was sure of it. Only when the results of the MRI came back negative from the orthopedist did I begin to suspect it might be something more serious.

"If it's not a nerve in my back, then what else could it be?" I asked my internist.

He said it could be a number of things, but I shouldn't worry about it. Numbness comes and goes.

"Could it be MS?" To my surprise, that was the first thing I asked.

He shook his head and laughed. "Whenever anyone gets numbness in their feet, they always jump to MS."

"I don't," I said. "My dad was a doctor. Doctors' kids learn that if you wait two weeks, whatever is bothering you will most likely go away. If not, take penicillin for a week and you're better. I don't jump to worst-case scenarios."

"If it would make you feel better, I can send you to a neurologist and schedule some more tests. But as far as MS, it's really unlikely."

"Unlikely, why?" I asked.

"Because of your age. And because you don't have any vision problems. That's usually the first sign."

For some reason, even though my vision was fine at that time, his reasoning didn't comfort me. Something within me knew otherwise. It was like when I was diagnosed with breast cancer. When the mammogram technician told me that if the films showed any abnormalities, I'd get a certified letter, I knew I'd find that letter in my mailbox. Two days later, I did.

I had no prior history of breast cancer in my family. I nursed my three children, which made the odds of having breast cancer slimmer. I was always concerned about good nutrition and exercise. When it came to my suspicions about MS, this same intuition rose up within me. (If only I had come to the truth about my life not being my story sooner, I would have seen these changes as signs of a challenge to come, a challenge meant for my own good. But back then, that perspective wasn't within my scope of vision.)

"Could it be MS?" I asked the neurologist during my first visit to him in October 2007.

His reaction surpassed that of my internist – and not in what I'd call a good way. "Oh, you women always think the worst. There's a hundred other things it could be, but you've jumped to the top of the list and are going about this the whole wrong way."

I stared at him. "If you knew me," I said, "you'd know that I don't overreact when it comes to illness. If anything, I go the other way. But I just have this feeling."

He shook his head and rolled his eyes. "Feelings? My advice to you is not to mention your thoughts about MS. You'll end up looking like you're paranoid. We'll go about this logically, step by step. I'll order tests to rule out other possibilities. You should have come to me first instead of trying to figure this out for yourself."

I stared at him, but this time I kept quiet. I left his office with four scheduled tests, including MRIs, blood tests, urine analysis, and, if necessary, a lumbar puncture. The results of these tests would take time. However, in the end, they would either rule out or confirm a diagnosis of MS.

Three days before Christmas, my neurologist called and told me he wanted to see me. I knew why. I followed him to a room toward the back of his office. He sat on the edge of he examining table, and I sat on a chair against the wall across from him. He told me that, unfortunately, the tests did confirm that I had MS. He didn't look at me. Instead, he sketched out this line graph with his blue ballpoint pen on the crinkly examining table paper.

"With MS, you start up here, at 100, and then it's a downward slide to zero. No one knows how the slide will go, but there's no turning up once you start that slide."

I stared at his squiggly line and then asked, "How old are you, doctor?"

He looked surprised. "Fifty-eight. Why?"

"Well, then, according to your graph, you're more than half-way down that slope yourself." I grinned.

He didn't. "This isn't about age. It's about an incurable, pro-gressive disease whose course no one can predict."

After handing me a hard blue package the size of a small brief-case that contained all the information I would need, he walked me out to the front desk.

"So are you going to cry now?" he asked.

Stonefaced, I stared at him. "No. At least not now. Not in front of you."

When I got to my car, I hurled the hard blue case into the back seat. As I drove home, "Have Yourself A Merry Little Christmas," was playing on the radio. This one song always reminded me of my dad who died seven years earlier of metastatic melanoma. Even when my dad was alive, the last verse of that song never failed to squeeze my heart:

> *Through the years we all will be together*
> *If the fates allow.*
> *Hang a shiny star upon the highest bough,*
> *And have yourself a merry little Christmas now.*

I flicked off the radio and drove the rest of the way home in silence. Tears flowed down my cheeks like a bitter cold March rain.

HOW I LOOK ON THE OUTSIDE ISN'T ANY-WHERE CLOSE TO HOW I FEEL ON THE INSIDE.

JoAnn said please don't bring anything. She was looking forward to making lunch for me herself. And she couldn't wait to see me. I told her I couldn't wait to see her, either.

After I hung up the phone, I took a deep breath. I realized I had not been totally honest with JoAnn. A part of me really didn't want to see her. Yes, I wanted to be with her, to talk with her, to share stories. She always had a natural peace about her, an easy laugh. But in truth, I was afraid to see after nearly two years how MS might have affected her.

I had to bring her something, though. Something to make me feel less empty-handed. So I picked up some flowers at the grocery store: Japanese irises, stargazer lilies, white daisies, three yellow bud roses, and delicate baby's breath. When I got to her ranch house, I rang her doorbell, and then I waited.

And waited.

"It may take me a while to come to the door," she had told me on the phone. "But don't worry. I'll eventually get there."

While I was waiting, I looked at the cluster of ballet pink irises in the front of her house. She must have planted them years ago when she was healthy. Or else she had someone else plant them for her. Because from what she had told me on the phone, simple things like dressing herself or fixing her hair usually took most of the morning and wore her out.

During that phone call, she laughed when she told me about the common actions we take for granted. Like putting on jeans without losing our balance or buttoning a shirt in less than an hour. And don't even think about how long it takes to get in and out of the shower and blow dry your hair. Her laugh, though, was not one of those fake, "Don't you feel sorry for me?" laughs. It was genuine: "This is how my life is now. My life, which used to revolve around counseling students, dancing, and taking care of my husband and daughter."

I stared at one of the irises. How complex yet beautiful it was, with its strong stalk and gentle, drooping petals. Inside, the stamen reached out from even deeper pink petals, the flower's center protected and open so that it could both give and receive.

I remained caught up in the complicated beauty of the salmon irises when the front door opened. JoAnn beamed when she saw me, her cheeks pinker and her eyes brighter than the perennials outside her front door. She was clutching onto a four-wheeled walker with a red seat and hand brakes. I took a deep breath. Then I bent down and hugged her fragile frame and felt her spirit unexplainably strong.

"I'm sorry to keep you waiting in the heat," she said.

"I'm sorry it took me so long to come see you," I said.

Seeing this beautiful dark-eyed woman primarily confined to her home, I wanted to get down on my knees and beg for her forgiveness. To confess to her what I really was sorry about: that cowardice kept me away because I didn't want to see what MS could do to someone who once danced effortlessly.

But then she said, "I'm just glad you're here today," and I knew there was no need for explanation or penance. My absence was a result of the choices I made yesterday. Today, I chose to come here. And for JoAnn, today, right now, this one moment, was all that mattered.

In that moment, too, JoAnn showed me how vital living in the here and now is as far as accepting any suffering we encounter. All of life follows an up-and-down journey in which we can feel peace and forgiveness only in *this* moment. Only in *this* right now. Only in *this* inhale and *this* exhale.

For in clutching tightly to the past and all the baggage we accumulated along the way, we feel shame, regret, guilt. In fact, during my drive to JoAnn's house, I thought back to my last trek through the woods at the Abbey and my one-week hiking adventure in Scotland. I could not envision any of those precious moments ever coming back to me again. In that looking back to what had been, any peace in my heart was shoved aside as longing and regret bullied their way in.

What is it that Euripedes said about unhappiness? "There is something in the pang of change more than the human heart can bear: unhappiness remembering happiness."

That pang struck deep within me when I remembered and thought – no, I was sure – that the best days and moments in my life were behind me. I was only fifty-six, but my best days of teaching were over. My possibilities for a new career in nursing were over. My best days of being an intimate part of nature were over. My best days of being a wife were over. And due to my medical condition, no man, I was sure, would ever knock at my door, eagerly awaiting me to fall into his loving arms (which, on my unpredictable, Scarecrow legs, I quite literally might have done.)

On the other hand, in looking ahead – even by a minute – I lost sight of the gifts right in front of me. In place of love and gratitude, I felt fear upon fear, bitterness added to self-pity. Fear especially controlled me. Could I make it from the produce aisle in the supermarket to the cereal aisle and then on to the dairy aisle without my right leg dragging behind me like a wounded Civil War soldier? Some days I was so afraid of trying to get that far I went without my staples of plain yogurt and granola. Oranges and spinach would have to do.

Even more than the immediate everyday fears was the terror brought on by all the "what ifs" and "what thens": What would happen tomorrow if today I couldn't walk from the produce aisle to the dairy aisle? What if a day came when I couldn't get out of bed? If I did get up, would I fall down the stairs? Or trip on them on my way back up? If the MS progressed, what use would I be to anyone? What if I ended up a burden tucked away in some white-walled institution? What would happen to me then?

In projecting my life into the future, I felt the very real power and evil of fear. I learned that fear begets fear. That it's an untamed, greedy monster that preys on your tiniest doubt, your unconscious worries. Being afraid is like having cancer where hideous cells multiply by the millions and help themselves to healthy places in the body where they don't belong. These cells don't care about you. They are only out for themselves. On those really bad days when I hung on to the grocery cart for dear life, I'd come home filled with paralyzing fear and feeling more than a little sorry for myself. Looking back (again, not staying in this one moment), I realized I had taken for granted the simplest of things: jumping in and out of a car without using both arms to help haul in my wooden legs. Not worrying about getting the key into the backdoor so I could make to the bathroom in time.

One time, as I frantically struggled with the back door key, warm urine flowed down the legs of my jeans. In that moment, I flashed back to the laughter of my first grade friends who witnessed the one and only time I soaked through my green and blue plaid uniform skirt. Even though there was no one around now to see my splotchy jeans, I felt enormous shame and humiliation for being one lowly (and not so pleasant smelling) human being who couldn't even manage what used to be an ordinary, natural act.

Keeping my own worsening MS moments to myself, I followed JoAnn into her kitchen as she carefully maneuvered through hallways and widened doorways to the kitchen. On one wall in the foyer, I noticed a stunning red, orange, and blue oil painting of three female dancers locked arm in arm.

"That dancer in the middle, is that you?" I asked.

She smiled. "Yes, that's me."

Not that *was* me. But that *is* me. Inside herself, where it mattered, JoAnn knew who she was. As for me, I could hardly remember my real inside self these days. Before MS came into my life,

I had mostly focused on the exterior Lorraine. How I looked and what I did defined me. Now, I, too, was in the middle somewhere. But as to who I really was, a brightly colored painting hadn't been created yet so that I could see.

As JoAnn slowly made her way to the kitchen, she talked about how glorious the sky looked today. "This room is my favorite," she said pointing to the den with high, bay windows off the kitchen. "I sit here a lot. It is amazing to me how every season has its own beauty. Even in winter. Even on the stillest day, when you don't think anything is happening, something is always happening." She looked up at me and laughed. "Guess I sound as if I've gone off the deep end, huh?"

I grinned. "No, you sound like you know what life is about."

She laughed again. "Me know what life is about? The only answer I'm sure of these days is, 'I don't know.' But thank you for your kind words. And thank you, too, for those beautiful flowers. There's a vase in the cupboard above the stove. Could you reach it for me?"

I detected no pity in her voice about asking me to do a simple task she could no longer manage. No embarrassment, either. Just an asking about a practical matter that was out of her reach. How long had it taken her to reach this place of asking? Asking and receiving – the two requirements of an open heart. I was in a place where I had managed to shut out both.

While I arranged the flowers, she shuttled back and forth from the kitchen counter to the table, which she had already set with white cloth napkins, china plates, and crystal water glasses. In the center of the table was an arrangement of white and red roses. My wildflowers paled in comparison.

"Would you move those roses to the den?" JoAnn asked. "The ones you brought are so beautiful. How did you know stargazer lilies are my favorites? No matter where you are in a house, you can smell their sweetness."

I set the perfect roses on a table in the den. Then I paused to look out at the sky where puffy white clouds floated like overblown rafts on a clear blue river. Once I got home today, I would still be able to put on my walking shoes and go out. At least for a block or two. My eyes filled with tears. It was so sad to me – "it" being the way JoAnn was filled with such remarkable grace. A grace which made me feel unworthy to be in its presence.

Although I swept away the tears before joining JoAnn at the table, she noticed the emotions I was trying to hide.

"Don't," she said. "It's just the way it is. And really, I consider myself one of the lucky ones."

"But how do you do it?" I looked into her deep brown eyes. "Here I am, still walking, getting out most of the time when I want to. Still teaching, even though there are days I'm not sure I'll make it through. And yet with all the abilities I still have, there's not a day I don't wake up and wish this away."

JoAnn handed me the platter of strawberries, wheat crackers, and thinly sliced cheddar cheese.

"I used to wake up like that, too. Some days I still do. But now before I get out of bed, I make myself focus on all I have. A loving husband. A healthy daughter. Enough money to hire a driver and go to any doctor I choose. Just think of all the people in this same situation who don't have any of these resources. How do they survive each day?"

"Many don't," I said.

She nodded. It's no secret to anyone who has done research on MS that 20 percent of people stricken with this disease find it so emotionally and psychologically unbearable that they end their own lives. Also, most of the medications are so outrageously expensive that if you don't have a good health insurance plan you have no choice but to go without.

"I know how depressing it can be," JoAnn said. "But whenever I feel sorry for myself, I think of people who have it so much worse. Children with cancer. Teenagers committing suicide. Parents who have lost their children to addiction. All those mothers and babies dying in wars they never asked for. Read the front page of the paper. Listen to the news. Every bad news story is ten times worse than what I'm struggling with."

She was right. I knew that. But I wasn't in a place yet where I felt grateful for my condition compared to others'. My heart wasn't completely locked shut, though. If you'd ask me if I had the chance to give this MS to someone else and be free from it, would I? Honestly, I would answer, "No." I couldn't think of one person, not even the one or two people I was happy not to be around, to whom I would pass off this disease. Not anyone.

For the first hour or so, JoAnn and I compared our MS symptoms. She never had double vision. "I can't imagine how I would manage that," she said.

She told me problems with bowel and bladder control. I told her I didn't know how she could manage that. She talked about all the doctors she had seen, all the medications she had tried. All the appointments with specialists in Boston's finest hospitals.

"In the beginning, with every new visit, every new medication, John and I would get our hopes up. This time it would work, we said. But I've been through everything so far. And I know for myself that nothing is going to change for me. But for you, it's different. You have never looked better. We won't see a cure for MS in our lifetime, but this disease isn't going to get in your way."

"But JoAnn," I argued, "how do you know? How I look on the outside isn't anywhere close to how I feel on the inside."

She looked at me with those intense brown eyes. "I know. And no one can say for certain how and when this disease progresses. But it came to you later on in your life. You won't end up like me."

"How can you be sure?" I asked again.

She shrugged and smiled. "I can't say for sure. But I just have a feeling you're going to be all right."

Then she added, "And now, let's not talk about this anymore. We have so many other things to catch up on. How's Emily? Where is Joe now? And what is Jeff doing?"

Gladly, we left our focus on MS behind. Like two old friends, we spent the rest of our time together talking and laughing about other matters: our children, politics, current events. "If only someone asked us," we concluded, "we could solve all the world's problems."

When 3:00 came around, JoAnn said she was getting a little tired. I told her I couldn't believe how late it was and that I had to get going, too. She smiled. I sighed. Then we were silent. Her acceptance of her MS was beyond me. Was it that she had had more time to accept where she was? Would I, with time, come to this place of acceptance? Was the adage true that time heals all wounds? If so, then why do so many people still hurt years and years after the initial wounding has ended?

I didn't know the answer. It would be a few months before I would hear Father Damien at the Abbey, but I already suspected that healing had to do with something much greater and less transitory than time. Love, I suspected, might have something to do with fixing those deep wounds.

One thing I did know, though. When I left JoAnn's that summer afternoon, my prayer had changed. Instead of asking God to keep me from being like JoAnn, I asked Him to give me the grace to be more like her.

I asked in good faith. But with fear and anger still filling up nearly every corner of my heart, I didn't have enough room to receive the healing grace I was being offered.

MAJOR SHIFTS HAVE TO HAPPEN WITHIN THE LAYERS BEFORE THE SURFACE CAN CHANGE.

After visiting with JoAnn and promising myself to cultivate gratitude for what I have been given instead of what I may have lost, here's the sad truth of our humanness. Mine, at least. What one means to do and actually acting on that intention might as well be as far apart as the earth is from the sun.

Perhaps you hurt someone because of something you failed to do. Like visiting your elderly aunt who can't drive her push-button Dodge Phoenix anymore because of her poor eyesight. You always liked Aunt Agnes. Every summer, you remember, she made a special chocolate cream pie with extra whipped cream and walnuts. The whole dessert, just for you.

But you grew up and your own life got too busy to take her for a walk or a ride even though she lived an hour away. It was too far out of your way. Sixty miles.

From time to time you thought about her and how special she made you feel during your awkward teenage years. Then one day when you felt a little down and lonely, you realized how hard it must be for your aunt to be so alone all the time. You connected your own suffering to hers and finally realized how happy it would make her if you spent an afternoon with her. But your new-found awareness couldn't help Aunt Agnes – or you, either – unless you chose to get in your car and travel down to visit her. In other words, in order for change to happen, you had to act.

As the truth gradually unfolded in front I me, I realized that to change even the simplest pattern in my life became a major struggle with the One who kept trying to get my attention. The One who kept trying to make my life easier by offering to carry every one of my burdens.

Maybe you, too, have a hard time with change. I'd wager that every day most of us put our right shoe on before our left one. We also brush our teeth in the exact same motion we've done since we were in kindergarten. We all fold our hands the same way, too, either left fingers over right fingers or vice versa. If we aren't aware of these daily ingrained habits, then how can we even begin to understand the ways in which our larger patterns control us?

For me then, while I tried to believe that Someone else was lovingly writing my story, actively following along with the plotline was another matter altogether. To change in a drastic way then, some deep fault in me had to get out of line so that great shifts would happen not only on the surface but within the layers of my self as well. In other words, within my real self. The real self My Author knew far better than I.

I'm stubborn. I still wanted control. I insisted on proof in order to trust completely: "If this story is really written for my own good, then send me one little thing every now and then to help me believe. Let me walk without wobbling. See without stumbling. Write without weakening. Not just for an hour or a day but for an entire week. Then a month. Then ten years."

Positive changes that I could see and feel. That's what I wanted. And what did I hear back each time I made another demand?

A ripple of laughter followed by, "How many times do I have to tell you? Don't be afraid. Come on, Lorraine. Make that leap of faith from knowing to doing. My arms are strong. I'll catch you. I promise."

But me of little faith. While I really did intend to be more accepting of my story, the actual getting to that place remained as daunting as jogging across the country and back in my bare feet.

Why did everything suddenly feel so difficult when I had felt such peace at the Abbey? Such reassurrance with JoAnn? How had I slipped back into the murky company of fear and doubt? Why had I lost my faith in the goodness of this story?

I couldn't sit around despairing over my numb feet and double vision. So that fall, I made the decision to go back to teaching. In order for my life to have any meaning, I had to do something. I mean, isn't that what our Western culture teaches us? We are what we do, right? And if we don't have a job title, then what good are we? (Funny, but now that I think about it, not once in my ten years of going to the Abbey did anyone focus on what I did.)

Two weeks into September, though, I contracted infection upon infection. With each new ailment, my leg muscles took on added inflammation and my vision worsened. When I went to my class on the third floor, I clutched the railing and took one step at a time while students flew past me in fluorescent flip-flops. Every noontime before I went home, I sank down into an empty student desk until I found the strength to stumble back down those steps. But once down the steps, could I make it across the parking lot to my car? It was never not a challenge for me.

Most afternoons when I made it back home, I collapsed on the couch. I remember calling my daughter, Emily, after one class in October. I had another sinus infection, and that day I was so dizzy I could barely stand up. I admitted to Em, who also taught college, that I was afraid I wouldn't make it to the end of the semester.

"Don't worry, Mom," she reassured me. "Thanksgiving break comes in four weeks. Which means you only have twelve classes left. I know you'll make it," she said.

Em was right. Besides her encouragement, I'm sure what helped me get through the remaining classes was the fact that I really loved my freshmen students, and I loved teaching the literary theme I devised for both classes called "Sounds of Silence." In essence, all the readings and writing assignments centered around when one should speak up and when one should stay silent. Going even deeper, we'd aim to uncover reasons why people stay silent when they should dare to speak and why they surround themselves with noise when truth is often heard in silence.

("Where'd you come up with that title," an exceptionally outgoing student named Joe asked me on the first day. He had an easy smile, and I could tell by his eyes that he asked the question out of genuine curiosity.

"It's a Simon and Garfunkel song," I said.

Joe and the other seventeen students stared at me as if I had been resurrected from the Dark Ages.

"Come on," I said, smiling. "One of you must know that song. It topped the charts in the 1960s."

The students shrugged and shook their heads. Then Joe threw me another curveball: "Who are Simon and whatever that other weird name is anyway?"

Now it was my turn to stare at them in disbelief. Didn't they ever unplug their IPods and listen to an oldies station? Didn't their parents share their music with them?

"They were one of the most popular duos in the '60s and '70s. I know you've heard their songs," I insisted. 'Homeward Bound'? Nope. 'The Boxer'? Huh? "OK, 'Mrs. Robinson' from the movie *The Graduate*. I know you've heard that one. Coo-coo-ca-choo. . ." Actually, no, they hadn't. I didn't even bother asking them about "Peace like a River" or "Bridge over Trouble Water." Unknown to them, they were going to be experts on those two poems/songs when we reached our last sections on prejudice and war.

Now that I think back on those classes, I realize the tremendous irony of that theme I had chosen. Here I was, passionately talking with these college freshmen about the courage to speak out and the courage to face their own fears so that they could connect with others and themselves on a deeper, more significant level.

And here I was, more frightened and more discouraged than ever. Not once in those fifteen weeks did I ever talk with them about having multiple sclerosis. I even went so far as to ignore the first essay in the book, which was written by a woman confined to a wheelchair because of MS. This piece would have been a perfect springboard for students to talk and write about their own personal challenges, physical and otherwise. But I refused to include it because I knew I'd have to raise the question: How do we usually react when we see someone who is disabled?

I predicted what the students would say: "We look away and pretend we don't see them."

Then I'd have to ask the follow-up question: "What are the reasons we look away?"

And I knew that answer, too, because it's how I felt myself: "Maybe we're afraid that we could end up like those people."

I was now one of "those people." I believed that if others knew I had MS they would look at me as being helpless and useless. Who could blame them? At that stage in my journey, that's how I saw myself, too.

Still, if I had had the courage to choose that essay, I could have helped my students understand that someone using a cane or a walker or a wheelchair is a person, too. A father, a mother, a brother, even a teacher. Revealing my own journey with MS might have helped them realize, too, that we never know what someone else is going through until we go beyond appearances and take the time to listen to someone else's story.

But I kept silent. I suppose most people would say that students don't need to know about their teachers' personal lives. It's like a doctor/patient relationship. We need boundaries, which necessarily set up people as patients and students as numbers. That's how it usually goes. And usually, that's how I taught.

But not always.

When I felt my own life experiences might help my students understand a deeper truth in their own lives, I briefly shared my own stories in connection to our readings. Such sharing, I found, removed many of the barriers that interfered with trust, especially when it came to students sharing their writing with me and being honest with themselves and each other.

For example, in this class, I offered a few details of my father's struggles with alcoholism when we read the powerful essay by Scott Russell Sanders, "Under the Influence." After hearing one of my memories, students opened up and connected with their own experiences.

"My uncle killed himself and damaged his whole family by drinking." This, by a young man who, unlike the majority of college freshmen, refused to touch alcohol at all.

"My dad was a mean drunk. You know, throwing around things. Saying mean things. Like if I got an A-, he'd yell and say I didn't try hard enough. Then he'd open up another Bud. But lately, I think he's drinking less. At least he doesn't seem as mean to me since I left for college." This, by a young woman who missed nearly every Friday class because she spent Thursday nights partying too much.

Toward the end of the semester, when we were reading *A Lesson before Dying,* a powerful novel by Ernest Gaines about prejudice, injustice, and complicity in the South, I shared my experiences in rural Mississippi during my many visits with my son Joe. Joe taught for seven years in the bleakest, poorest part of that state, the Mississippi Delta, which Jesse Jackson aptly named "America's Ethiopia."

My firsthand accounts of prejudice and despair among the poverty-stricken black population stunned my students. Most of my freshmen came from small towns in the Northeast that were practically void of minorities. They had little exposure, other than a few mandatory lessons during Black History Month, to the historical struggles of African-Americans and their present-day inequalities.

Through sharing my experiences, my students began to see that Americans living in the Delta remained virtually invisible to the rest of the country. The majority were poor, black, and many of the children didn't know their fathers. Most of these same children didn't graduate from their public high schools. Even people who lived in other parts of Mississippi couldn't give you directions to the Delta's sparsely populated towns that are nothing more than pinpricks on a map.

Towns like Ruleville, Indianola, Shelby, Alligator, Drew, Shaw, Merigold, Sunflower, and Money.

As pleasant as these last three towns sound, don't let their names fool you. Merigold is a tiny town split by an unused train track. It lies hidden behind a highway that scurries past this Delta town on its way down to more important places. Like Vicksburg or New Orleans.

Sunflower also sounds like a beautiful place to live. But like Merigold, it finds itself divided by a rusty train track that separates, for the most part, black residents from their white neighbors. Sunflower also has a library the size of an outhouse. I'm not sure if it's still open. And if you blink going down Highway 49, you'll miss the green and white sign for this town. You also won't see any sunflowers growing here.

Then there's Money, Mississippi. Its name reflects fame and success. But this place, an empty space north of Greenwood, looms as a ghost of a town whose few remaining buildings will probably be buried beneath weeds in a few years.

In my class, I introduced my students to Emmett Till, a black teenager from Chicago who visited his relatives in Money during the summer of 1955. One afternoon, Emmett went into a country store and supposedly whistled at the white seventeen-year-old female cashier. Because of that whistling, a group of white men brutalized Emmett's body beyond recognition before tossing his remains into the Tallahatchie River.

Even though the men boasted of their heinous actions, they were found innocent within forty-five minutes by a jury of their peers: twelve white men. The murder of young Emmett and the glaring injustice in our legal system helped ignite the beginning of the Civil Rights Movement.

But I'm sure you're wondering: What does the Mississippi Delta have to do with my story? Ironically, as I found myself moving closer to the edge of despair that winter, in a little town a stone's throw away from Emmett's murder my Author placed a new purpose to my life.

This purpose came in the form of a precious blue-eyed, two-month old baby named Sam. But in the three months before I learned what Sam had to teach me, I went through what St. John of the Cross calls the dark night of the soul.

Beneath the shroud of those dark nights, I nearly lost myself.

FROZEN UP FROM MY HEART TO MY SOUL

Whose woods these are I think I know.
His house is in the village, though;
He will not see me stopping here
To see his woods fill up with snow.
My little horse must think it queer
To stop without a farmhouse near
Between the woods and frozen lake,
The darkest evening of the year.
He gives his harness bells a shake
To ask if there's been some mistake.
The only other sound's the sweep
Of easy wind and downy flake.
The woods are lovely, dark, and deep,
But I have promises to keep,
And miles to go before I sleep,
And miles to go before I sleep.
("Stopping by Woods on a Snowy Evening," by Robert Frost)

Most everyone knows this poem, especially people here in New Hampshire where Mr. Frost wrote, farmed, and taught for a few years. People say this is a simple poem, an easy read. I read somewhere that Frost wrote these four stanzas late one evening, hardly changing a word. For any poet, any writer, that's nearly impossible – to have a piece come out like that as if you had nothing to do with its birth but be present.

Years ago, I committed this poem to memory because of its smooth rhythm and lulling rhyme scheme. Before my son Jeff bought a red IPod Shuffle for me one Christmas, I walked three miles every night, in rain, snow, or under stars, breathing this poem in and out to myself. I did that for seven years, which meant that reciting this poem became as natural for me as breathing.

Especially when I felt weary going back up a long hill, I'd go to the poem, pull it out of my memory, and get back in step to the rhythm: Unstress, stress. Unstress, stress. With the poem as my internal walking stick, I steadied myself and let go of the world for a while.

After I learned I had MS, though, that poem took on a whole new meaning for me that wasn't quite as simple as many might think. In fact, the way I saw it, Frost's popular poem contained unsettling contrasts and paradoxes. White flakes float against a thick, inky background. Green pine trees huddle next to a frozen, colorless lake. The narrator – I picture an old man – rides alone through a barren landscape that reflects his inner loneliness. Only one word – "lovely" – shows the beauty of the snow-filled woods.

Following that hint of beauty, though, Frost uses two words to show the true nature buried beneath the snow. Woods in winter are "dark and deep." Woods anytime, but especially at night, are not for the faint of heart. They hold fallen limbs. Dead leaves. Creatures too tiny to see. Specters both real and imagined.

In winter, even the smallest sounds in the woods disturb us. The lonely crunch of our own footsteps. The crack of a branch behind us. The hoot of a distant owl. The rush of a wind that holds not one ounce of sympathy for us as we push our way against its powerful, invisible force.

Understandably, most reasonable people don't trot out into the woods alone, especially not in a blizzard. No lights guide the way. No warmth awaits us. Even if the sky is clear and the stars shine like pinpricks of light through an ebony velvet cloth, who can see them? The tall pines block the view. The stars, these pines seem to state smugly, belong to them. If we want to see stars, we've clearly wandered into the wrong place. Go find an empty field or somewhere else with a sky opening.

The more I thought about it, the more this seemingly simple poem raised troubling questions for me: Why did the narrator come to these woods on a dark night? Not just any dark night but the darkest night of the whole year? Was life too much for him to bear? Did he come here to lie down in the thick woods beneath the thick snow where all the burdens and cares in his life would vanish once he vanished, too?

In the end, though, no matter how much the narrator might have despaired, he did not go through with his plan to stop for good in these dark woods. He lingered for only a moment. Then he followed the cues from his horse and kept going because, as the poem says, he had promises to keep. In the end, he had the good sense to crawl out from beneath whatever plagued him and chose to remember his connections to others.

Getting out of your own sorry way and thinking of others: That keeps people going when the world, as another poet said, "is too much with us."

But the winter I stopped teaching, my journey's last stanza was not going the way of the narrator's in the poem. I'm sure the Writer of my story wanted me to pick myself up and move on through the storm. Or maybe not. Maybe the Writer wanted me to go through that deep despair the old man felt. If that were the case, the Writer did a superb job of handing me a chapter (or a period) filled with a depression so smothering I found myself gasping for air.

For the first time in my adult life, I wasn't doing what I loved. I wasn't raising my children and sharing intimately in their lives. After twenty-one years, I also wasn't teaching. Then in the second week in January, I was notified that the local column I had written for twenty years for the local newspaper was no longer viable.

"We just don't have room for the type of writing you do," the new editor e-mailed me. "It's not local enough."

Love, loss, sorrow, friendship, death, life, injustice, joy, connections, education, peace, family, nature, gratitude – none of these issues were local enough? Really?

I wrote back two words to the new editor: "All right."

After meeting nearly 1,000 weekly deadlines, the ending to this chapter in my life actually did feel all right. I had simply lacked the courage to make this change for myself. So the door to raising children was closed. As was the road to teaching. As was the road to writing my column, which, no matter what else was going on in my life, at least kept me fixed on a deadline each week.

"That editor's an idiot," my youngest sister Annie said, dwelling on the editor's curious reasoning. "But look on the bright side.

Now you can do your own writing. Even if you can't do some of the other things you used to, you can always write. You always have that."

But the thing is, when we're out there in those deep, dark woods, we've purposefully ventured out there because we don't want to do anything. We don't want to be with people. We don't want to look at the bright side. We seek out the darkness to hide what hurts us.

For me, I also didn't want to write. Not a word. It was like my insides were as frozen up as the ground in February.

That's how I felt for nearly three months. Frozen up from my heart to my soul. All of me, locked up like an antique silver heart charm without its key. Locked up and useless. Like I no longer mattered. Like nothing mattered. All the passion and joy I had known before — being a mother, a teacher, a writer, a good friend — all of these things seemed as if they belonged to some other woman I barely recognized anymore.

Some other woman once found joy in simple things: a red cardinal perched on a snow-covered pine branch. A front yard newly carpeted with a foot of fluffy snow — perfect for making snow angels. The first stars that crept out from behind thick clouds, signaling the end of a three-day blizzard.

The stars now? Many nights I despised them. What good were they to me if I could no longer go out and look at them? On the nights I did dare to go out, I stared down at the ground, watching my every step, for fear of falling. That fear was real. More than once, especially the closer I got to home, I'd miss a step and fall down on the side of the street. It was as if a shadowy stranger had sneaked up behind me and yanked on both of my ankles.

No doubt it would have done me good to dare to look up once in a while. To put away the fear and just breathe. Or to go out and stand in the front yard where I could see the stars. Or to sit on the old redwood bench by the bare maple tree in front of the house and listen to what the quiet on the outside might be trying to say to me on the inside.

But fear in those dark times kept me from hearing anything that could help me. I even doubted that the people I loved in my life remembered me. What good was I to them now? They didn't need me. They had their own lives to live. Lives which included working and being with others and doing whatever they pleased. Lives where they could go out walking day or night if they wished and never once worry about crashing down on the ice and cracking a rib or two.

After I might have gone out to do a few errands each day, I came back and collapsed on the blue leather couch in the den. I never turned on the TV. I never listened to my favorite music. Not even Eva Cassidy's "Over the Rainbow." Especially not that. In my hopeless state, that song never answered why bluebirds could fly where I couldn't.

I didn't even read. I just lay there, looking at the bare azalea branches outside the window or staring blankly at the sprayed-on popcorn beads on the ceiling.

Physically, I felt as if I were unraveling like a loosely knitted sweater being pulled at both its beginning loop and its last knot. My spirit, too, which had never failed to uplift me, was now so full of darkness I couldn't feel gratitude for anything. Not even for waking up that morning.

As convinced as I was in my dark state that no one cared about me, in reality that was not the truth. My three children phoned all the time to see how I was doing. So did my closest friends. So did my husband even though he had moved on in his own life.

People still cared. But being in this place of darkness, I didn't have enough light to feel or see or believe that. In fact, whenever anyone called I always mustered up a happy voice full of phony cheer to convince that person I was all right.

"Is there anything I can do for you? Like bring you over dinner? Or come over to talk?"

"No, really, I'm fine."

Then I'd hang up the phone and be angrier than ever that this person who called didn't come over with homemade chicken soup and keep me company. Crazy, huh?

Crazy, yes. For how could people know how I felt if I didn't tell them the truth? How could they know how desperate I was, how close to despair I felt, if I didn't share my depression and anxiety with them?

Despite my reluctance to share my trials, I did have two people who knew the truth of what I was going through. At any time, I could call my friend Ginger. She lived right down the block and was always at home, too. Ginger used to teach until her third battle with ovarian cancer made her too weak. Compared to her disease, what right did I have to feel sorry for myself? None at all.

But Ginger never made me feel as if my MS were any less threatening than her cancer. Sometimes, on the spur of the moment, we'd go out for a light lunch or a comedy at a matinee. We saw It's Complicated twice. No matter how we were feeling, we always ended up laughing about one thing or another.

I remember Ginger once said, "We must be two really amazing women because from what I've seen only the really wonderful people in life seem to get these horrible things."

During one lunch when Ginger could barely swallow and I could barely read the menu, we asked how we could have gotten so sick when we always made sure to take good care of ourselves: exercise, eat right, laugh a lot, help others. We half-kiddingly concluded that we hadn't done enough bad things in our lives, and that's what caused our troubles.

"The next time around," Ginger said, "I'm going to booze it up. No more half a glass of wine twice a year for me. Give me a straw and the whole bottle."

"I'll join you at the bar," I said. "We'll devour plates of greasy French fries and cheeseburgers and afterward, we'll go outside and chain smoke Camels." We both laughed.

I also had one other person in my life who was, to quote a "A Case of You" from Joni Mitchell's *Blue* album, "as constant as the Northern Star." Like the North Star, communication between the two of us didn't depend upon words. It existed like gravity, an invisible force that kept me grounded. In fact, in the ten years I knew Father Roger, the pastor of Holy Cross Church, I never directly told him about the troubles in my personal life or the depth of my pain. But as every parishioner knew, Father Roger had a gift for knowing.

Perhaps because of his experiences as a counselor in the jail for twenty-three years, his lifelong passion and talent for painting, or from his own personal dark nights, this humble man, crippled with arthritis, connected with other people's lives as if he, too, had once lived them. Many in the parish saw him a mystic. From all the synchronicities I experienced in his presence, I saw him that way, too. (Father Roger, though, completely denied the title and would hear none of it whenever anyone mentioned it. Which proved to us all the more what a holy man he was).

During my darkest times that winter when my frozen smile and "it's only a little limp" fooled everyone else, Father Roger sensed the truth. Once he phoned during an unexpected ice storm that paralyzed New England two weeks before Christmas. The storm raged through the night, cracking down huge tree branches along with uprooting whole trees. By morning, ice-covered pine trees barricaded the streets, broken branches damaged homes and cars, and impenetrable inches of ice downed all power lines.

Now not only were my insides and the outdoors frozen up, but for five days, my house had no heat, no light, no water. No power. I kept logs burning in the fireplace, but that small fire only gave off three feet of warmth in a house that had grown too big for me.

On the night before my power miraculously came back on (most people lost power for more than two weeks), Father Roger called as I huddled in front of the last logs burning in the fireplace and left this message:

"Hi, Lorraine. It's Father Croteau. I'm just calling to encourage you. You looked a little bit down yesterday, and I didn't blame you for all the stuff that's happening. But I have an hour of power right now (he laughed) before it goes off. One electrician in the parish has connected my phone to a generator, so that's good at this point here. And things are working out. Well, I know that everything looks bad, but it'll get better, Lorraine. I'll be with you spirit. OK. I'll talk to you later. Bye bye now."

With his one and only hour of power, Father Roger called me. That night, his words gave me hope when I most needed it. He said my life would get better. That I was not alone. No other words could have warmed my heart better than those.

So I did have people who came to my aid. But those people were few mainly because I chose not to share my diagnosis of MS. I'm not sure why. Maybe I harbored too much of that dangerous thing that "goeth before the fall." That thing that gives the ego its power. That thing called pride.

Or perhaps I couldn't come to grips myself with the idea that I had this disease. I always saw myself as the one who lifted others' burdens. The one who had soft shoulders for others to cry on. The hospice volunteer who sat on the end of the bed saying, "I know it's hard. I'm so sorry."

I saw myself as the one who would answer the phone in the middle of the night and stay connected until the person on the other end found some sense of peace. Or hope. When my sister Annie was stationed in Iraq as a nurse anesthetist, she'd call me whenever the war began to chip away at her inner shield.

"Maria was only two-years old." Annie called one night sobbing from an ICU medical tent north of Baghdad. "I thought she was going to make it. You would have loved her chubby little legs and cheeks and her big brown eyes. For three weeks she held on. I thought she had gotten through the worst of it. But the burns were too deep."

That morning, I, the one answering the phone at 3:00 a.m. wasn't the brave one. It was Annie who was open and trusting enough to let down her guard and admit the truth of how hard it was to be in this war.

I didn't work in a war zone like Annie. But a deadly battle raged within me like a wind-swept forest fire. Unlike Annie, though, I was too terrified to speak. Too proud to admit that I felt helpless. Too numb to feel deeply. Too overwhelmed to think clearly. Too weak to reach out. Too consumed with my own pity to see that so much of what I was feeling was due to the dismal perspective I had chosen for myself.

In fact, I was so blinded by darkness during those winter months that I didn't even remember I had a choice as to how I could view this disease. I didn't even remember that while Someone else was writing this story, I had the choice to trust in this truth and enter into this story with hope.

With the perspective of darkness I had wrapped around myself, I refused to ask for help. My daughter Emily said she would come home in a minute if I needed her. "Really, Mom, do you want me to come home this weekend? I can book a flight tonight. I can be there by he morning."

I knew she would cancel her classes and come if I even hesitated. But I told her no. I was all right, really. I had just been one of those days. As much as I wanted to be with her, I didn't want to burden her — or anyone I loved — in the state I was in. Pride, self-pity, fear.

My younger son, Jeff, who lived in Washington, DC, called at least three times a week. He told me about his work, but in the end, he always brought the subject back to me: "I know you're going to turn this around, Mom. So don't give up. You're going to beat this thing."

With feigned hope in my voice, I'd tell him I knew I was going to get better, too. It was just a matter of time. And then I'd hang up the phone with tears in my eyes because I didn't believe one word of what I had said. In truth, my hope was down to an ember so faint I could barely see or feel it.

Joe, my son who now lived in Mississippi, usually called in the early evenings on his way home school. He never failed to ask how I was doing. I'd tell him I was all right. That some days were better than others. Then before he could ask for more details, I'd quickly switch the subject to his students. As a middle school principal, he had more stories in his one day than he had time to share.

But mostly, Joe shared with me the new and most precious gift in his life and in the life of his wife, Catherine: their infant son, Sam, who was born in the Delta on January 15th, Martin Luther King, Jr.'s birthday.

"Really, Mom, I'd tell you if he looked all scrunched up and scrawny like most newborns," Joe said when Sam was born. "But he's beautiful. Really beautiful. If Catherine decides to go back and finish the semester teaching, can you still come down in March to take care of Sam? If you're not feeling up to it, that's all right. But you know we'd all love to have you stay with us."

I told Joe and Catherine that of course I would come. To have the chance to watch my first little grandchild grow from baby tears to belly laughs, how could I miss that?

So the third week in March, I packed up one big purple suitcase, and I flew to Memphis where Joe picked me up. Within two hours, we were in the little town of Ruleville, right smack in the heart of the Delta.

Did I have my doubts as to whether I could make it three months down in Mississippi caring for little Sam? To be honest, I did. I rarely struggled with double vision anymore, which was a blessing. But I still felt tired and weak, like I had been KO'd in a boxing match.

I still couldn't walk very far. I still had trouble with my balance and dragged my right leg by the end of the day. But something about this decision felt right. For the first time in months, I felt as if I were finally listening and following along with the script that had been written for me.

In the days and weeks before I made the trip down South, I prayed and prayed and prayed to have the strength to care for Sam. Sam and Joe and Catherine needed me.

More than that, though, I needed them. I also needed things to change in my life. Externally, but more importantly, internally.

EITHER HEAL ME OR SEND SOMEONE WHOSE LOVE WILL HELP ME GET THROUGH THIS.

Externally, the change happened by leaving my home and going to a place where I felt the anonymous peace that comes, at least for me, with being an outsider. For some people, being alone in a different place makes them uncomfortable. Lonely, even. Since my husband and I separated, though, I had to learn that it was all right to go out to eat alone. To go to a movie alone. To buy one piece of haddock and not worry about someone noticing how my shopping cart contained only enough food for one person's dinner.

Externally, I also physically came out of isolation and became a part of a larger community that included my son Joe, his wife Catherine, and their eight-week old son, Sam. The place where I found aloneness and peace instead of separateness was the deepest part of the South, known as the Mississippi Delta.

How ironic that I had to go to another forgotten place to begin to remember who I was.

After flying to Memphis, I knew Joe and I had arrived in the Delta when I realized that we had been driving south on a little two-lane highway and had not seen another car go by for ten minutes or more. I also knew I had arrived there when the brown, flat landscape on either side of us melted into the hazy blue sky, like a somber Rothko painting. Suddenly, like a hiker coming out of the woods, I had a 360-degree view of the world around me. For miles, I could see everything. Every tree left standing alone in a field. Every cloud sighing by. Every red-winged blackbird flitting in and out of newly plowed fields. All of those natural creations and all the nothingness in between.

I had forgotten how open it was here. Also how barren. As we made our way to the tiny town of Ruleville, I sensed a certain stillness that felt both unsettling and settling. Now, though, I was somewhere where, if I chose, I could live within these opposites with much less fear than I harbored in those dark winter days back home.

"You won't believe how much Sam's grown since he was first born," Joe said as we got closer to his house. "He sees things now. Really sees them. I know every new parent says this, but really, Mom, Sam is so amazing. He seems to know so many things. It's hard to explain. But you'll see."

I knew what Joe meant the moment I held little Sam all snug in his blue blanket and looked into his blue eyes. No fear lived there. Just wonder and an innocence that believed all in his world was right and good.

And in his first two months of life, it was.

LORRAINE C. LORDI

Joe and Catherine may have been first-time parents, but they had learned to put away the books, support one another, and listen to Sam. They knew what most of his cries meant now. Usually he was hungry, but sometimes, he just needed to be snuggled and held. In those times, they held Sam up close to the strands of miniature Christmas lights that glowed day and night around their living room ceiling.

"Sam really likes the lights, so even though it's March we're leaving them up," Catherine said.

Such a simple thing. Plastic Wal-Mart Christmas lights. And yet when Sam got fussy, all we had to do was hold him up in our arms and walk around the room so he could see those lights. Although he didn't know what he was seeing, he gazed at each one as if it were an angel that he not only remembered but knew by name.

None of us can remember those firsts in our lives, like looking at our first tiny white light. Or the first time our lungs filled with air. The first time someone held us. The first time we cried. The first time we laughed. The first time we felt hungry. The first time we saw colors – only black, white, and red for the first few months, experts say.

But then can you imagine what it felt like when we woke up one day and saw green and blue and purple and gold? Such a glorious burst must have made us feel as if we had entered in a new world. Imagine, too, how it felt the first time someone looked at us as if we were the most precious gift on earth. A miracle so breath-taking that all paled in comparison to this one, perfect little person who hadn't done one thing but be born.

This one special person, a long time ago, was us.

Regardless of how we look on the outside, regardless of how we feel on the inside, that precious person still lives within us somewhere. Only once the world moved in, we forgot all of those firsts — from dust balls in the corner to a shard of sunlight on the mud room floor — that reassured us that everything here was created for us. And that all is well.

All is well. If we truly believed these three simple words, all would be well, indeed.

"All" — meaning everything in our lives. The bruises, the blushing, the shadowed valleys, the glorious mountaintops, the algae ponds, clean flowing rivers, the hugs along with the hurts. The loves and the losses. The dawn and the dusk.

"Is" — meaning right now. This one precious moment. Not tomorrow. Not yesterday. Not an hour from now. Not even a minute earlier than this. But this in-breath. This out-breath. This now that is the only time in which we really are. This "is" which is eternal and never-ending.

"Well" — meaning a place deep and full of water to keep us alive and refreshed. Alive and good in the sense that this is exactly how it is supposed to be. In this place of wellness, there is no fear. No illness, either. We're not half or three-quarters. We're whole and well-cared for. We're well-loved.

How often we forget those three simple words in the concrete chaos of the world around us. Being human, I suppose we have to. But we can also sense a part of us that is a spiritual being. In order to fully realize this other half of us, we have the choice to tune in, enter the "cosmic dance" as Thomas Merton said, and become one with all.

Living this truth is easy to put down on paper. But from what I've learned, it's so hard to remember our united spiritual selves unless we constantly stay here, in this one moment.

Being in the moment. For eleven weeks, that's the gift I was given when I was with Sam. Physically, I didn't feel any better, but being present with Sam and caring for his needs helped me worry less about my future or rue my past.

"What do you do all day?" my mother once called to ask me.

"I watch Sam," I said.

"But what else do you do? Do you get out? Meet other people? Write?"

I told her no, I didn't write. Sometimes on the weekends or when Catherine got home I went to the Kroger's in the not-so-big town of Cleveland. Or I retreated to my room to read or rest. After the school day ended and on the weekends, Joe, Catherine, and Sam needed to spend time adjusting to and delighting in their new roles in their family.

But I had the privilege of spending the weekdays with Sam. Paying close attention to him. When he took a nap, I did. When he woke up, I woke up and fed him. Then I held him and sang to him. Or I put him in his little lamb swing and spent the whole time looking at him.

I sat on the couch two feet away from Sam and marveled at the way he moved his lips. Opened his eyes. Kicked his legs. Drooled and burped. I noticed his every little eyelash, his fine blond hairs on his round Charlie Brown head. I delighted as he tried to figure out his fingers. Did they really belong to him? I rooted for him as he struggled to put his thumb in his mouth and hit his pink chubby cheek instead. "Don't worry, Sambones. You'll find your mouth soon," I said.

But my greatest joy erupted when Sam learned to smile. A wide-mouthed, jack-o-lantern smile that melted my heart every time he sent it to me. And what did I do in return? I made the same silly wide smile back. And opened my eyes as wide as he opened his. And I laughed. The day he laughed back (no, it wasn't gas), I took a picture for his mom and dad and spent the whole day smiling from the inside out.

I know for Sam these simple moments are forgotten, buried somewhere in who he used to be before he could turn over, touch his toes, crawl, or walk. But for me, having someone's face light up whenever I walked into a room made me feel unconditionally loved and accepted.

One afternoon when I was sitting on the couch watching the baby monitor a if it were the most compelling movie ever made (Sam was fast asleep), I recalled a prayer I had said during those dark winter months in New Hampshire. It was a type of petition my dear friend Dyan, who has the faith to move stone mountains, urged me to make.

"We don't ask for enough because we don't believe, really, that God wants us to be happy," Dyan said. "So try this. Believe He really loves you. Then take the "either – or" approach. Think of two things you feel you need and go for both. You'll get one of those prayers answered. In time, I believe, you'll receive both."

Based on Dyan's suggestion, my prayer during one of those dark nights went something like this: "Lord, if you're still out there, either heal me or send someone whose unconditional love will help me make it through this."

As I watched Sam sleeping, I realized: my "either-or" prayer had been answered. Slowly, I was working on letting go of fear and healing internally. One prayer answered. In addition, I had been given that unconditional love I asked for: Sam. At three months, this little baby loved me as much as I loved him. I also realized that had I not had MS, I would still be teaching and would never have had this chance to remember the real power of love, a power so strong it thawed my frozen heart.

It didn't matter to Sam if I couldn't take him out in his stroller for very long walks or dance around the room with him in my arms as I sang to him. He didn't know my legs wouldn't let me do those simple things. And he didn't care. All he knew was that someone was there, always, acutely aware of whatever he needed and wanted.

He didn't think less of me when we got back from a short walk one day and my legs barely got us both up the three brick steps and into the house. I sat on the couch with him and tried to sing "Somewhere over the Rainbow," but when I got to the part about bluebirds flying I choked up. Sam looked up at me and smiled as if to say, "I think your song is beautiful, Nanna."

So even on those days I felt weak and discouraged, Sam's innocence reminded me that life was a rare and precious gift created by Someone who loved me more than I could imagine. Like little Sam, all I had to do was trust that everything in my life was taken care of by someone who loved me.

"How was Sam today?" Joe asked me this same question the first few weeks he came home from school.

"Perfect," I always said.

"No, really, Mom. How was he? Did he get fussy? Did you have a hard time getting him to sleep?"

"Nope," I said. "He was perfect."

It was the truth. Even if Sam fussed or cried, which he seldom did, he was perfect in my eyes. After a while, Joe quit asking, "How was Sam today?" He knew what my answer would be. That answer stayed the same until the day in late May when I had to pack up my one big purple bag and head back to New Hampshire.

How was being with Sam, really? Every single moment was perfect. Really.

* * *

As much as Sam shone as a bright light in my life during those eleven weeks, I also had moments when I felt discouraged. When I was around Sam, I could live in the moment and forget about what I could no longer do. But sometimes alone in my room, I fell back into feeling a tremendous longing for the healthy, energetic person I used to be.

Once, sensing my disappointment, Joe told me that maybe if I concentrated on what I could do instead of what I couldn't that would help me feel better about myself. His advice was spot on. But at the time, I had too many moments, especially when I was out walking, when I drifted back to the past and focused on the days when my legs could carry me for miles and miles without stopping.

Most nights after dinner while Joe and Catherine bathed and put little Sam to sleep, I went out for a walk. Usually, I only made it past six or seven humble houses to the end of the block. A few times, I made it to the end of the block and then all the way around an empty plot of land that used to be a Little League field (for white players only). In total, that walk measured less than a quarter of a mile. But since it was the farthest I walked without the fear of fall-ing, it felt like a victory to me.

But there were nights when I couldn't get much farther than the old oak tree behind Joe's yard. I'd lean against that tree, facing an empty field, and look at the stars. Or, if a storm had come through that day, I'd stare at the amazing bursts of lightning putting on a show in the far-off horizon. If I let go of fear, I could come out of myself and feel the enormity and mystery not only from the energy of the spectacular light show but even of the tiny chirps of crickets rising out of tall weeds.

One night, when the sky stayed gray and empty, my right leg kept me anchored to the ground. Since I couldn't walk without stumbling, I leaned against the oak tree out back and heard an owl hooting. Even though I couldn't see it, I knew it was close enough to see me. I stayed out there for nearly an hour listening to that owl's voice break through the darkness as if it ruled the night. I suspected it was trying to tell me something. Only I had no clue as to what it was saying.

When I came back in, Joe asked how my walk was. I didn't want to admit to him that I made it only to the tree out back. So I shrugged and said I heard the most amazing owl hooting into the night. Joe knew me too well, and he could sense how discouraged I was. But instead of pressing me about where I had been all that time, he simply said, "I've heard that owl before, too. I think it lives in a tree not too far from here. But I've never been able to see it. Sometimes, it hoots all night."

I heard the hoot owl every night after that, but I never did see it.

Another mystery to me was this small white church sur-rounded by a cluster of trees about a mile across the field. In the seven years I visited Joe, I had never seen anyone venture into that church. But every year, the unused church looked clean and fresh and ready for company.

During my stay in Ruleville this time, I had one goal: I wanted to make it to this little church and its adjoining graveyard that appeared out of nowhere in this field behind Joe's house. In years before, I could jog out and back to that little church without breaking a sweat. This time, I wanted to prove to myself that even though I couldn't run, I could surely walk to this mysterious plot where faith and death remained under the protection of a circle of trees.

As the weeks passed by, though, that oasis in the field seemed as far out of my reach as that hoot owl. Still, I was determined to get there. I couldn't let fear keep me from trying. So one hot Sunday afternoon, I put a leash around Joe's collie-mutt mix dog, Peanut and headed out toward that church. Peanut often came with me on my walks. Joe said Peanut needed to get out, but I think Joe knew I needed this shaggy auburn dog to pull me forward when I needed pulling. Which happened more often than not.

Halfway across that sun-baked field, though, I realized that while I may be able to get to that church, I could never make it back. Fifteen minutes into this walk, my legs already shuffled like they were filled with bricks. I tugged on Peanut's leash, even though I could tell he was disappointed. We turned around as he gently pulled me toward home.

As we made it out of the scorched clay field and onto the street, I saw a group of three young black boys on their bikes and one smaller boy on foot passing by. They all stopped. Fear filled their young faces. Except for the small boy who wasn't on a bike. I knew what they were afraid of: Peanut.

"Don't worry," I said to the boys. "He's a really nice dog. Come on over. You can pet him. He won't hurt you."

The three boys on the bikes vigorously shook their heads. "No, Ma'am," one said, "dogs around here, they is mean. They bite."

Another boy on a bike looked at me and asked, "Ma'am, what you doin' goin' off in that field anyways? Don't you know snakes is in there?"

I laughed and said I wasn't afraid of snakes. That I knew what poisonous snakes looked like and that most snakes I saw around here were harmless. In fact, snakes are afraid of people, I told them. The three boys on bikes looked at me as if I had stepped out of that field from another planet.

"No, Ma'am," that same boy on the bike shook his head, his eyes wide as the moon, "all snakes is dangerous. If I saw one, I'd chop it up into pieces with a knife. That's what we do."

Snakes and dogs and water. In this deep part of the South, these three concepts, I've learned, scare African-Americans like ghosts in the night. It makes sense. In their blood, in their memories, perhaps in the cells of their unconscious, they see real danger in these natural objects from the way their ancestors lived. And died.

I knew better than to argue with the boys' history, so I smiled and said it was a beautiful day for riding bikes. Just then, Peanut spotted a squirrel in the yard across the street. He raced off toward that squirrel like a rocket. I knew the boys would think Peanut was coming after them, so even though his leash burned in my hand, I held on to it as if it were one of those white-hooded ghosts.

Peanut's passion and energy proved too much for my legs, though. Still clutching his leash, I crashed down on my right elbow and knee and then flat with my forehead to the pavement. The three boys on bikes took off as fast as their little legs could pedal. The one small boy on foot stayed right next to me.

As I struggled to get up he asked, "You all right, Ma'am?"

I looked up at him. His head partially blocked out the sun, creating an aura around it. I looked into his light brown eyes. He looked into mine. Our eyes shared the same color. I quickly got to my feet so he wouldn't worry about me. He handed me my sunglasses that had skidded into the middle of the street when I fell. Then he stood quietly next to Peanut and me until I steadied myself on my feet.

"I'm all right," I said. "Thank you for staying with me."

"Yes, Ma'am," he said quietly.

I started walking (limping, really) toward Joe's backyard. The slender young boy walked down the street in the opposite direction of his friends on their bikes. After a few steps, I turned around. I wanted to thank him again. But he was nowhere in sight.

Tears welled up in my eyes. Not because of the ache in my elbow or the pounding in my head. But because of that one boy. His faithful presence reminded me of that one winter day when I trudged through the snow to go to confession. I knew I was walking with something holy then. This time, the grace came from a child. Grateful for this precious reminder in my time of need, I had no doubt: The Writer of my story had sent this boy's protective spirit to be with me. Until I fell flat on my face, though, I couldn't feel or believe that I walked hand-in-hand with such sacred company.

Call me crazy. Tell me the blazing noontime sun had fried most of my brain. You'd be right.

The sun had indeed melted away the part of me that thought too much. The part that kept trying to reason and rewrite this story. The sun had also melted away the remaining ice chips in my heart. Maybe now, thanks to what Sam and that little boy had shown me, I could finally give up my will and hand my story over to the Real Author no matter what lay ahead.

If, that is, I held on to those two simple gifts Sam and the boy kept alive in their hearts: trust and love.

I'M NOT THERE YET . . .

Down the road from the Abbey, March 19th, 2011

So I came out on the porch at this cottage to have my lunch after Mass, a Mass in honor of St. Joseph the Carpenter. I sat out there on a faded plastic chair with a small blue plate of three delicious Triscuit, tomato, and cheese sandwiches. And a tall glass of ice water. With all the woods around me, I felt as if I had found the perfect spot in a treehouse.

While I sat there, I saw a dozen or more bright red cardinals, redder than the reddest rose, circling the trees around the porch where I was sitting. I had never seen so many cardinals in one place. Then I realized: They were flitting around from tree to tree because they wanted those black sunflower seeds I had filled in the hanging feeder on the porch yesterday. But they were too afraid to come to that feeder while I sat there.

How could they know I had put those seeds out there for them to enjoy? How could they know I wouldn't hurt them? I was just watching them and delighting in their beauty and how they made every tree branch theirs. How every bit of the sky was theirs. How little effort it took for them to move their wings and soar from branch to branch.

Even though I wanted to be a in their company for lunch, too, I came in off the porch and watched from the window as they sang and flew and were being what they were meant to be. If only they knew I was just watching out for them. But how could they know that? We existed on two totally different planes, the birds and I.

Which is why, we, too, have such a hard time trusting the Creator of our stories. We can't presume to know a heart and mind so alien to ours. But when we look back, when we stop to listen, we see clearly that this loving Force always puts out even more food than we need. Most often, though, we are too afraid to receive it. Too untrusting. We? What I really mean here is me.

That journal entry I wrote jumps ahead to nearly a year after my stay in Mississippi. As had happened too many times to mention in these past ten months, that which I never imagined became a wondrous part of my story. Like having my neurologist agree to change my medications. Since switching medications, not once in the past nine months had I battled an infection or taken a serious fall. Little trips now and then but no broken ribs. I was far from running again, but walking straight and steady with single vision — that was beyond what I could ever have hoped for last year.

And another most wonderful gift. On the spur of the moment, I journeyed back to the Abbey for a weekend retreat. Spur of the moment, really? Clearly, it was a gentle push from my Guide who wanted me to partake in the gift of being on holy ground the moment winter melted into spring. The very moment when darkness and light balanced each other out perfectly.

The retreat house, I knew, was closed for spring cleaning. The monks, too, were on their private Lenten retreats. For two weeks, they took a break from their everyday work assignments. Even monks need naps sometimes.

But since I was so close to the Abbey (I was spending the winter in Asheville, North Carolina where Joe and Catherine and Sam now lived), I decided to take a long weekend and travel to Geth-semane. So what if this time I had to spend two nights down the road from the Abbey because carpets were being scrubbed? I was welcome at all of the prayer services.

Plus, as I wandered through the retreat center, I had the priv-ilege of having the whole place to myself. The kitchen where I picked up some small boxes of granola and a few oranges. The library where I sat and reread some of my favorite Merton pas-sages. The garden where I walked among bare trees and a brown landscape. No bees or crickets and few joyful birdsongs filled the air this time of year. In this midpoint of Lent, the silence here had never been so silent.

To my great delight, though, I got to meet with Father Damien for an hour two days in a row. Both meetings were unplanned (at least we didn't plan them). And both times, we sat, talked, and walked together like two old friends instead of the strangers we had been three years earlier.

"What a surprise to see you!" he said when I met him in his office. "Where are you staying?"

I told him I was right down the road in a one-room cottage at Bethany Spring.

"Do you have anything to eat?" he asked. "You know the cook isn't here these two weeks."

I laughed. "Don't worry. I'll get a few things at the store. I'll be fine."

He shook his head and laughed. "You seem fine. Happier than the last time I saw you. How's the MS?"

"It's still there," I said. "But I feel better. Many days, stronger. Some days, not the best. But now the good days outnumber the not-so-good ones. I'm not complaining."

He shook his head and smiled at me. Then we talked about the weather. How hot it was for this time of year. Near ninety, which felt more like the times I came at the end of August.

"Things are changing," Father Damien said. His eyes were light but his words heavy. "A big shift is happening in the world right now. Everything will converge at some point soon."

I sensed that whatever he knew about life rising and converging was not meant to be shared now. Then he smiled and switched the topic to his growing up days in Holyoke, Massachusetts. I never knew that he spent his childhood there. I told him that western Massachusetts had always been one of my favorite spots to visit. The mountains, the rivers, the naturalness of it all.

"I'm not surprised you like it," he said. "It's a beautiful area, sacred ground in many ways."

He also told me about his missionary trip to a convent in Indonesia where he felt completely lost at first. "I lost track of which day it was because of the time difference. I missed my flight by a whole day. So here I am, a big tall man in a country of shorter people where I didn't speak the language trying to explain that I need to get to this convent. But I also didn't have any money and didn't know how to get in touch with the Sisters. Now if I didn't have Someone watching out for me, I'd still be in that airport trying to find a way out."

We both laughed. I shared with him my story about how I got lost, too. As I entered the back roads of Kentucky, my GPS conked out. Yes, I had also brought written directions with me. But since most of the back roads were unmarked, I drove around in circles before somehow finding a narrow road that linked to Trappist Way.

"Like you in that airport, I have no doubt that Someone else finally took over the driving so I could get here. Now let's see if that Someone will lead me back out of these woods in two days, too."

Without having to say it, we both realized the paradox of a true pilgrim's journey: Getting lost is a natural part of this adventure, and the only way to get where we need to go is to keep trusting that Our Guide will eventually lead us to the right path "though we may know nothing about it," as Thomas Merton wrote.

Since we were sharing a few of our more humbling moments and laughing at ourselves, I told Father Damien about how when I made my first visit to the Abbey ten years ago, I thought angels were going to swoop down from the heavens and flutter all around me.

He laughed. "So did they?"

"No," I said. "At least not that I could see while I was there. Not until I was on the plane ride home did I realize that angels danced around me the whole time everywhere. In the flowers. In the clouds. In the wind. In the chants. In the sunsets. In the heat lightning. In the other retreatants. In the silence. Especially in the silence. But because I had this one idea already set in my mind as to what would happen during that trip, I couldn't see the angels at the time."

"We all think too much," Father Damien said, pointing to his own head. "We think that what we have in our minds is the truth. If we only listened to what our hearts tell us, we'd never get lost."

"I know I think too much," I said. "And I second-guess my Author a whole lot more than once in a while. As far as finding joy in this story written for me when my legs and energy give out – to tell you the truth, I'm not there yet. I may not even be close."

Father Damien's response surprised me: "We aren't meant to find joy in suffering. We just have to trust that for whatever reason, this is what's meant to happen in our story right here and right now. The joy comes later."

"But if we really believed that everything in our story was meant for our great happiness," I argued, "then wouldn't we be joyful despite our suffering?"

He shook his head. "Having faith that Someone else controls our lives doesn't make life any easier for us. But faith in Another's plan does bring us peace. And hope, which keeps us waking up each morning grateful for yet another day and trusting all that will unfold within it. You know, today has been a great day for me. My knee doesn't hurt. And here we are, talking. And the Abbot is away for two weeks. So after I dropped him off at the airport this morning, I came back and took a nap. So far, a great day."

I laughed. "So when the cat's away, the mice will play."

"Naturally," he said. Then he stood up. "Let's take a walk. Look at that day out there. It's like summer."

We left his office and walked out to a spot in front of the Abbey with one long bench and two chairs. We sat quietly on the wooden bench. Father Damien looked up to the cloud-dotted sky to his left, comfortable in his own thoughts. I looked straight ahead at the bare branches on the tree in front of me. I listened to the wind. And breathed. And followed the thoughts in my heart.

This journey is already set out before me whether I can see it or not. The meaning of this journey, though, is not what I could find in the dictionary – the idea of packing up my bags and traveling to a certain destination. In fact, this journey story is not about packing up anything, I realized. How does a person know what to bring along if she doesn't know where she's headed?

As Father Damien said, it all comes down trust. Trust, like those cardinals waiting on tree branches by the porch and knowing they will eventually be given what they need. Trust, like Father

Damien waiting for someone to come rescue him in a foreign country. Trust, like me following all those winding back roads.

The whole idea of "this story isn't mine" journey requires ripping up my road map (which doesn't recognize unmarked back roads anyway) and tossing my own plans into the wind. The only journey worth taking is about giving up total control and letting Someone else guide us through each day. (Which now makes me wonder whether Someone else planned all along for my GPS to fail on those unmarked country roads. I'm betting so).

Time and time again whenever doubts have plagued me, I've been given more than enough signs to embrace the sublime mystery of this journey we call life. But having faith in Someone Else's greater plan is still, after all this time, a mighty struggle for me.

Oh, on days when I can walk thirty minutes without my legs dropping like anchors, trust and gratitude gush through me like water in the desert. With hope-filled joy, I exclaim, "Hurray! I like this plan of Yours after all. I trust you – now that I'm feeling better."

But on those days when I can't muster up the energy to step over the smallest rock in my path, I wonder if traveling this journey of faith is worth it. Am I just kidding myself that these trials in my story really do serve a greater purpose? Sometimes, I wonder.

I don't believe I am alone in this wondering. Nearly six thousand years ago, Lao-Tze, the founder of Taoism, spoke of the difficulties in embracing the idea of a journey in which we essentially travel blind. As one translation of his famous quote reads, "A journey of a thousand miles must begin with a single step."

A thousand miles. Who can see that far into the distance? Who can see beyond this one moment in time? No one. As my friend Jean wrote to me last month when she heard of her youngest son's cancer, we are all one phone call away from the life we had planned changing plans on us.

Yet no matter how many perils we face along the way, we *must* dare to set out in the darkness on this road. We *must* believe the journey serves a greater purpose.

We *must* – or else what?

Or else we – at least I – remain paralyzed in fear. A river covered by ice. A heart without a heartbeat. A subject without a verb. Shocking as this may sounds, if I don't choose to travel this road whose end I cannot see, I am nothing more than a corpse taking up valuable space on this earth.

"It's almost time for Vespers." Father Damien interrupted my thoughts. He smiled and stood up. "Are you ready to go?"

I looked at him and grinned. "I sure hope so."

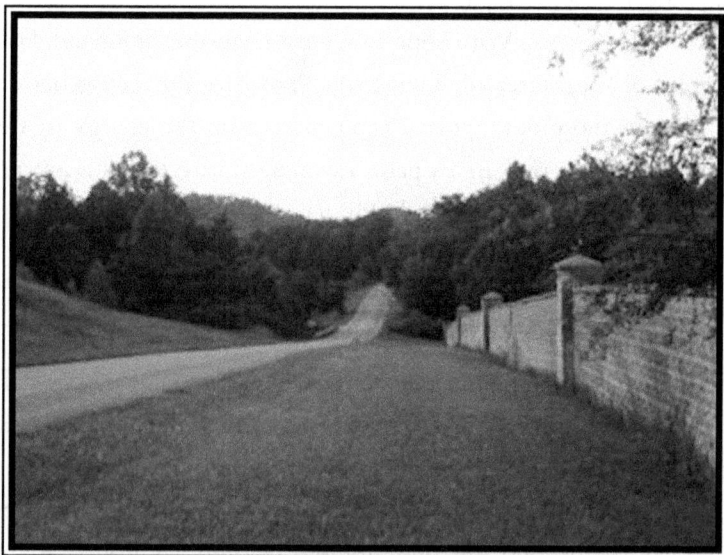

BUT AT LEAST
I'M STILL HERE.

Starting and stopping and starting again. Deleting and revising and deleting again. For seven weeks, that's how this last chapter has been going for me.

I've tried dozens of beginnings. I've forced out endings. As soon as I finished each one, I tried to kid myself into believing that it felt right. But every time I began and ended again, something in my heart let out a little cough, "Uh-uh," a clear sign that nope, this twelfth and last chapter was not anywhere near where it needed to be yet.

During all the struggles of writing this last chapter, I thought I was listening. But as I've learned, while our thoughts may trick us, that which lies within the heart always tells the truth. My heart kept trying to tell me what I needed to write. But I wasn't listening. Instead, I spent countless hours trying to sculpt this last chapter as if I were the sculptor.

You'd think I would have learned by now.

But as the constant rewriting of this last chapter has shown me, that old habit of believing I controlled everything proved a hard one to break. After I accidentally (yeah, I know it was no accident) rediscovered one of my favorite poems one rainy afternoon, only then did I get out of my own noisy way and listen to a voice that knew better.

"*Listen,*
the heart-shackles are not, as you think,
death, illness, pain,
unrequited hope, not loneliness, but

lassitude, rue, vainglory, fear, anxiety,
selfishness."

In these six lines from Mary Oliver's poem, "When Roses Speak I Pay Attention," I recognized my all too familiar inner clouds that blocked the sun and moon from lighting my way.

Weariness. "I've been going over this stupid last chapter so many times, it's wearing me down. What the heck? I didn't even want to write this book in the first place."

Heaviness of heart: "Who am I kidding? I can't write a book when my heart feels so much sorrow now. So many friends struggling with personal problems. So many wars. So much devastation from floods and fires. So much pity for my own self when I jump out of bed and my legs feel like lead."

Pride and Selfishness. "This is MY book. I'm the one producing all the words. Hurray for ME!"

Fear and Anxiety: "What if no one likes *my* book? What if, in fact, they hate it? What if people make fun of *me*? What if writing *my* book has been a complete waste of *my* time? What if *my* book is just another failure in *my* life?"

Scared to the bones of writing *my* book? Really?

Time out.

Listen to what you're saying, Lorraine. Read these lines again. Then go back to the first line: "This is not a book I want to write." Got it now?

Yes, maybe. I believe so.

This may not be the book I wanted to write. But it is the book Someone wanted me to write. Someone else was in charge of the beginning, every chaper that followed, every spacing, every word, every photograph. And Someone else is writing this last chapter, too.

So if Someone else is in charge, why am I so afraid? I need to do what I did before. Shut out the senseless chatter in my mind and listen to my heart. Kick my ego out the back door for the ten-zillionth time. Let the Creator of this story help me out. In fact, I need to quit trying so hard and just let it be.

"Good choice to give that ego another swift kick. Now you can go back even farther. Go back to where this leg of the journey first began."

Go back – but not backward. That makes sense. So, back to the beginning. Was it three years ago when Father Damien's words shattered my heart open with "This is not your story"?

"That is a part of it, yes. But it's not the actual beginning. When and where did I first plant the seed for this book? Wait and listen to the wisdom in your heart, to the voice in your gut. Where did the mystery really begin?"

When I first was diagnosed with MS? Is that it?

"You didn't wait long enough. Quit thinking about the words spinning around in your head. Go back to the first image that unfolds clearly, slowly,

within you. Forget about time and space and what you want. Listen. Wait. Trust me."

A deep breath. When did I first realize that this was not my story? When, before being diagnosed with MS, did I come face to face with a challenge that was both unexpected and completely out of my control?

I closed my eyes and saw myself during my third retreat at the Abbey where I hiked up into the mountains and lost my sense of direction. I saw me, a middle-aged woman, ashen, wide-eyed, her face full of worry lines. I tried to stay hopeful: "This next turn will bring me to a path that looks familiar." But the farther I walked, the deeper I sank into the wilderness.

I finally had to admit the truth. Here, in these dense woods, I could possibly perish. I had no food. No water. No one knew I was here. Too weak to keep walking, I sank down on a rotting log and dropped my sweaty head into my hands.

That's when I heard, "Rest up. Then go a little farther and turn left. You'll find a clearing. There you'll find spring water. Once you're refreshed, follow the bells. They'll lead you back."

When my heart calmed down, I got up and followed those directions. Within minutes, I found that clearing. In that clearing, I heard the faint call of the church bells keeping track of the time at the Abbey of Gethsemani.

Gethsemani. Could the beginning of my journey be found within that one word? Within this one place?

"Yes. In the three central images of the Christian story of Christ in the garden, you'll find the beginning, the middle, and the end of this ongoing, never-ending process that makes up your story. But the answer is also found

*in every great story, written or spoken, in which an ordinary person comes
up against some challenge and triumphs over it.*

*"Oh, and one more thing, my dear. This story isn't really about you
and MS. It's about everyone's story and the process everyone goes through
on this journey called life. It's unique to each person and at the same time
universal. To overcome any trial we face, we all take the same three steps
designed to push us forward whether we know it or not. Steps that spiral up,
that spiral down — minute by minute. Breath by breath."*

I let go of trying to come up with the right words and focus
on three images that come into my heart's vision of the Christ
story that began at Gethsemani. A process some call the Passion. First, I see a middle-aged man dropping to his knees, beg-
ging to be released from what he is being called to do. After
sweating blood in the darkness of that garden, he comes to
accept the call to sacrifice his one life for everyone, believers
and nonbelievers alike.

Next I see a broken man, his head crowned with thorns, stumbling and falling under the weight of a wooden cross. After falling
three times, he finally reaches the place where he is crucified on the
very cross he accepted to carry. Lastly, after his friends run away
in fear, a new and transformed figure ascends from the tomb and
ambles down another road with his disciples. In his new form, his
friends fail to recognize him until he connects to them with their
sacred ritual: the breaking of the bread and the sharing of a meal.

In that first image of Christ, I see how we have to accept what
we've been asked to do by trusting in a plan greater than the one
we have in our little minds. It doesn't matter whether the call asks
us to make a great sacrifice like protecting our comrades in war or

to graciously accept the boring routine in our everyday lives like getting up with a sick child in the middle of the night. Every call matters.

Next, I see how after we accept the call, we have to actually do something in order to make change happen. Take action. That's the second step. Again, it doesn't matter whether we tiptoe inches in front of us or dive to the depths of the ocean. Whether we're strapping up to go to the moon or daring to speak the truth, every time we step out in faith, we move forward on the path.

Finally, after accepting and acting on the call, we ascend from our own trials and emerge in a new way. The change can be life-altering, like the addict who breaks out of a deadly habit and becomes a new person. Or the change can be invisible, like escaping the confines of a judgmental self to become a more forgiving and tolerant person. Whenever the perception changes, we enter into a new reality, seeing ourselves not as people who limp but as people who are loved. Because we are.

Accept. Act. Ascend. Three powerful words that have, as I look back on my story now, stood as the cornerstones of my journey thus far:

I accepted that I couldn't hike for miles in the woods. I actively took a seat in a small room and listened to truths a wise monk shared. I then ascended my limited viewpoint that had been blocked by trees and began to see the hills from a panoramic perspective.

Although I started out whining and bargaining and stamping my feet, I finally accepted the truth that I wasn't the One in control of my story. I returned the pen to my Creator and trusted in Her writing of the story. Because of that acceptance and choice on my part, I emerged a person with greater humility and gratitude.

I accepted how truly powerless I was in the midst of ice storms and darkness. I actively admitted my fear and uncertainty and admitted my need for others. I arose out of that dark night with a more open heart that was ready to be filled with light again.

I accepted that I could only push a stroller two blocks and that I could only make it halfway across a field. I came back inside and smiled with little Sam. I thanked the young boy who stayed by my side. I came out of my self-pity and recognized how fortunate I was to have such amazing encounters that lasted anywhere from three months to three minutes.

I accepted the fact that without my GPS, I had no idea where I was going. I continued driving around in circles, trusting that I would eventually be led to the right road. I arose out of my frustration and fear and arrived at a new place filled with hope, gratitude, and unexpected joy.

Reflecting on the past three years, I see with with greater clarity the never-ending process of this amazing journey. I also know without one bit of doubt that the One in charge of my story purposefully placed every person I encountered along the way as a source of compassion, wisdom, and hope. For as this One knew, I – and all of us – find our way back to who we are through the relationships in our lives, whether those relationships are fleeting or forever or fall somewhere in between.

On journeys entwined with mine, others answered their calls and took action to help me. When I was in danger of being swallowed up by sorrow and allowing MS to define me, my son Joe quietly sat down at the kitchen table with me and said, "You're still the same Mom to me."

From my daughter, Emily, I received gifts of practical, gentle words that comforted me without allowing me to fall into the trap of self-pity: "You'll be all right, Mom. And if you can't come see me this weekend, I'll drive down to see you. No problem. Either way, it will be fine."

I received deep-belly laughter from the humorous outlook my son Jeff offered to me: "As you, my Buddha Momma, always told me, the universe is conspiring for my happiness. Well, it's conspiring for yours, too. So go with the flow of the good karma. And don't forget to say Om."

From Father Roger who in the coldest, darkest winter never let my flame of faith burn out, I received the confirmation I needed: "Well, I know everything looks bad, but it'll get better. I'll be with you in spirit."

All of these words came at the exact moment I most needed a dose of hope and truth, which brought me to this new insight: I could choose to see every encounter as a chance happening or as a miraculous one. I chose to see the miraculous.

It was a miracle when my niece Lindsay sent me a shoulder bag she made from leftover materials the very day I needed a dose of seasonal joy. Inside the bag her note read, "Nothing about this gift is perfect. But I know you know how to love thru imperfections. Thank you."

It was no accident that the moment I fell down three brick steps, ripped my jeans, and banged up my left knee, my niece Casie called and left this message on my phone: "Hey, I just wanted you to know I'm thinking of you and love you so much. That's all!"

It was miraculous that my friendship with Ginger reached a new level of truth when I most needed her light. After battling ovarian cancer for six years, Ginger passed away three weeks after Easter this year. How blessed I was to be able to talk with her three times in the month before she took a final bow after the last act of her story here on earth.

"You're going to get better," she said to me.

"But I want you to get better, too." I teared up even though I promised myself I wouldn't.

Ginger smiled at me with her deep green eyes and said, "I will."

Without saying so, we both knew what she meant. In this story that is written for us but not by us, our faith in the Greatest One tells us the our physical end is not an end at all. It's a new beginning where we finally return to where we began. In this, the final step of our journey, we ascend to a love so far beyond our imagining it remains our greatest, most glorious mystery.

Once I embraced the belief that I had never been alone on this journey, I slowly came to realize that I was lovable not for what I did but for who I was. This truth, a hard one for me to accept, was reaffirmed whenever I focused on the simplest moments in the here and now.

Simple gifts like these two words: "You're precious."

A dear friend closed an e-mail to me seven months ago with these two words that reminded me: Even if I'm walking as stiff as the Tin Man or struggling with wobbly legs like the Scarecrow, it doesn't matter. I'm as valuable as a rare gem because of who I am inside of this body.

"Hey, look at Lorraine, y'all. She's got that downward dog butt up to the sky!"

So proclaimed Joe, the most joy-filled anusara yoga master in Ashevile, North Carolina. Because Joe knew: To those who can turn themselves into pretzel poses, mastering this basic position is no big deal. But to me, who couldn't bend down and touch my toes five months ago, having the strength in my arms and legs to get into this triangle shape signaled a major accomplishment.

In addition to unsurpassed compassion, my Author, I'm beginning to see, delights in mixing the silliness of life with the sublime. Like my rear end high above my head. The cardinal singing outside my window. The sunsets at the Abbey of Gethsemani blazing in rosy purples and golden whites. The full-face grin of a humble monk who winked at me and said, "You will, someday."

At the time, I thought Father Damien was talking about writing this book. But now I see a deeper meaning in these words. Someday, I will what? Who knows? As the non-author of my story, the possibilities remain endless as long as I go back to the the first part of the story and keep saying "yes" to whatever my Author instills in my heart. As long as I keep stepping out on a road whose end I cannot see. As long as I keep allowing the trials to change my life around and within me.

Yesterday, when my body felt especially achy and tired, I groaned and asked my Creator what I should do. In my heart I heard, "Put on your walking shoes and go out for a walk, Honey."

Going out for a walk was the last thing I had in mind. But I went out anyway. And for the first time in more than a year, I walked a mile without my legs dropping. An unexpected miracle to me.

During that same walk, I also realized that I have only fallen once in six months. That one time I fell down the brick steps. Three years ago, a fall like that would have thrown me into despair for days. This year, though, I listened to Casie's message, threw my ripped jeans in the trash, and went out to get a new pair of Levi's at the general store in Asheville.

Aha! In that seemingly insignificant fifteen-minute incident, I took all three steps in the journey process. I answered a call to trust that I was all right. I actively got up and walked back into the house. Then I literally got rid of an old part of me, my favorite jeans, and went out and bought a new pair.

I still have a long way to go in this story that has been written for me. I still have moments – too many of them – when I would much rather not have MS. But a funny thing. Three nights ago, my daughter Emily called. Toward the end of our conversation that flowed from the meaning of life and love into the next season of *American Idol*, I said, "Tonight when I was out walking, I realized that I liked myself more now than I ever have. Isn't that so strange?"

Strange, yes. But true. So what if I don't know where I am going. So what if I can't see what's going to happen next or where I am in this story now. Am I at the end of a chapter? The beginning letter of a word? Who knows? Amazingly, not knowing the answer feels fine to me. Because whatever is meant to happen next, I have to believe it's going to be all right. Sometimes, I even sense that it's going to be spectacular.

Why? Because the Author of my story and of your story, too, is Love. Who else would we want in control of our journeys? I don't know about you, but I can't imagine any power greater. So even though I am not there yet, wherever there is, at least I'm still here.

And for now, in this one precious moment, I can't imagine a better place to be.

www.ingramcontent.com/pod-product-compliance
Lightning Source LLC
Chambersburg PA
CBHW071003040426
42443CB00007B/645